Let Go

Accepting Who You Are Today
So You're Ready for Where You'll Be Tomorrow

DUANE S. MONTAGUE

ISBN: 9781980667759

DEDICATION

This book would not be possible without my wife.
She spent a year of her life next to a sleepwalking husband,
a man who was struggling with accepting who he was and letting go
of the past, however awesome and wonderful it had been.
If anyone has helped me learn what it means to *Let Go*, it's Robyn.
You'll see that as you read the book.

Thanks, babe.

TABLE OF CONTENTS

ACKNOWLEDGMENTS

Thank you to my four amazing kids:
Audrey, Austen, Autumn, and August.
Thanks also to my parents, Robert & Cherry,
my brother and sister-in-law, Douglas & Kara,
my sister, Lisa, my grandmother, Margret,
and my sister-in-law, Michelle.

I'd also like to thank Marion, Brian, Hannah, and Braden
for proving that there are friends who stick closer than brothers,
and for journeying with me.

Thank you.

FOREWORD

I originally wrote a short book on acceptance in 1997.

It was part of a series I created called *The Bear Necessities*. They had cute illustrations and simple thoughts and scripture to give people a quick read, an easy way to address some of the big ideas of life in a non-threatening way. (The character was named Eddy Bear. Hence, the "bear" necessities of everything from life to simple living to acceptance and grief.) I keep them on a bookshelf as a great memory of something I did a long time ago.

I recently realized I needed some advice because I was struggling with being okay with myself and where I was in life. I saw the book about acceptance and picked it up. The me from 20 years ago was dumb and didn't know a lot, but I said some good things.

I had a few *really* good things in there that helped me come to the conclusion everyone else around me had come to long ago: I was not good with acceptance.

I was holding on really tightly to the things in my past, both the good and the bad, and I wasn't ready for what might actually be coming in my future.

The cute bear illustrations seemed to nod and say, "Yeah, we saw this coming, buddy—you should have listened to us." And I should have. The 30 original thoughts about acceptance helped lead to this book. It's a bit of an adaptation of what I wrote 20 years ago—and a whole lot of new thoughts from a guy who has gone through even more in the last 20 years than I would have thought possible.

Four careers. One awesome marriage. Four amazing kids. Six different places to live. Three cats (one went crazy) and one beagle (which drives me crazy). Countless road trips, mini-vacations, and adventures to Disneyland, and way too much Diet Coke at times.

My honest hope is that you see that you're not alone.

Everyone struggles with acceptance. It's hard to find contentment and joy when you're in a "waiting place," and all you can think of is what will come next. It's not easy to be okay with who you are when you're struggling with old wounds and new fears. I understand because it's where I've been for the last two years of my life.

Maybe, like me, you're carrying a lot of baggage from the past.

The journey you're on is just getting started, and the suitcases of memories are going to get heavy.

Acceptance helps you lay them down and bring only what you need on the journey.

With faith, much reading in the Bible and other inspirational authors, a lot of encouragement, and several moments of wisdom from my extremely sensible wife, I'm finally, almost kind of, there. I can accept who I am. I can accept where I am and what I'm doing. I can see that I have a purpose.

All I had to do was accept who I am today so I could be ready for what was coming next.

All I had to do was let go.

Looking Backwards

This book is all about letting go. And letting go is not easy, because, from the moment we are born, we learn that when things look uncertain, we feel safer when we are holding on tightly.

Letting go of the past, accepting where you are today, and being ready for the future is not always easy. Sometimes you hang on to the past because you loved things about it. Like a well-traveled suitcase, it's battered and bruised but it holds a lot of memories you think you need for the journey ahead.

Perhaps you loved the role you had, or the friends you made. Maybe you have a hard time seeing who and where you're supposed to be today because yesterday was so good. The past is not always painful. The suitcase can be covered with stickers and luggage tags that remind you of happier moments and memories.

1

My past—like yours—has some really great moments.

I've been lucky enough to do some incredible things in my life, and it's easy to spend a lot of time relishing the good moments of my past. Getting married, the birth of my kids, road trips to National Parks, that time I was in a parade down Disneyland's Main Street—I have great things to look back at.

Maybe you're holding on to the past because you were hurt there. Someone wounded you, people betrayed you. It's hard to let that go because when you trust others, when you make yourself vulnerable and are let down, the pain goes deep.

I totally get it—I've been wounded pretty badly.

And I'm not talking about the time in 6th grade when I ran inside to talk to the teacher during recess because another kid called me short and I had to accept the fact that I was, actually, in truth, short.

I'm talking about the big wounds, the ones that take a while to get over. Sometimes they come from people that you care about deeply, and they are hard to recover from. Relationships can cause big time hurts—especially when it comes to matters of the heart.

Like the wound I got from the girl who broke up with me on our way home from a college choir retreat. Maybe it wouldn't have been so bad if we weren't driving a van full of our best friends back to the campus, which was four hours away. (Talk about your awkward silences.)

Long after college, I thought I'd found another girl, the perfect one. We both worked together and enjoyed it. She laughed at my jokes and I thought she was quite pretty.

Turns out that was also an unwise choice because she was younger, I was older, and she didn't get along with everyone in my family. At one point, she also tried to run me over with her car—I was never very good at reading signals from women as you may have guessed—and it was clearly not a healthy relationship.

When we broke up, I was heartbroken—again, because I was alone. It takes awhile to recover from love that is lost, and it's hard to let go of the wounds.

(For the record, I met the most amazing woman a few years later and we have been happily married for 20 years now, so even though I didn't do well at first, my love life turned out pretty good, I'd say. If you aren't certain, go back and re-read the dedication.)

But there are many other things that hurt us, too.

Lost relationships, lost jobs, lost moments. I've had friends who just stopped speaking to me one day. I lost one job I loved due to internal politics and left another one because the people I trusted to help my career never came through.

I just realized this may sound a bit like the Festivus episode of *Seinfeld*, so I'm going to stop the airing of grievances. "I've got a lot of problems with you people, and now you're gonna hear about it!" All that's missing in the book so far is the Festivus pole.

So, to avoid that, let me just say, I've been hurt, too. More than once, just like you. I've been there, the person sitting next to you has been there, and so has everyone else.

It's a horrible place to be.

But you can't keep looking backwards.

It's helpful to look in the rearview mirror as you drive, to see where you've been and the things you've passed. Try driving down the freeway that way, though, and you'll endanger yourself and everyone else and cause one of those accidents they used to show on the *CHiPs* TV show, where everything always ended with flying cars and explosions.

The only way to make it down the road is to look *ahead*. Maybe it's time to start looking there, because that's where your future lies. Ahead of you is where it matters. There's something right in the road ahead of you, and you better not miss it. Maybe it's the next big love, the next big adventure. Maybe it's just a day where you have to clean the toilets and nothing exciting happens.

Whatever it is, it's where you are now that matters.

The promotion you didn't get? Behind you.

The person who broke your heart? Behind you.

The _____ that keeps you _____?

That's behind you, too.

Whatever reason you have for holding on to the past, today is the day where you have to begin to let go. Accept who you are *today*, because yesterday is over, and God isn't saying *anything* about what tomorrow holds. Annie may have sung "Tomorrow! Tomorrow, is always a day away" but outside of a catchy Broadway classic, we aren't promised tomorrow.

It's *not* always a day away.

Trust me—you don't want to spend a year or more of your life looking backward, holding on to the past.

When the year is up, you'll realize how much time you've wasted and if you're nearing 50, you'll realize you don't have enough years left to waste.

The apostle Paul writes about this in his letter to the Philippians. After writing to encourage the Philippian believers to be joyful and rejoice in every circumstance, Paul reminds them that it's no good living in and hanging on to the past.

"Forgetting the past and looking forward to what lies ahead," he begins in chapter 4, verse 13.

Paul could easily look at the past, full of hurts and hardship. He's been lied to and lied about. He's had his motivations questioned, his sincerity doubted. He's been shipwrecked and dragged outside the city to be stoned and left for dead. If anyone has a reason to hang on to the past, it's Paul.

He goes on to say, *"I press on to reach the end of the race." (Philippians 4:14, NLT)*

He will forget the past and look forward.

Never mind what happened before, he says. It's time to press on and reach the goal. And what's the goal? Becoming who you were created to be.

Achieving the very purpose for which you were placed here.

All the good, all the bad, and everything else you've experienced? It's all happened for a reason.

Honestly, there's not a part of you that doesn't exist for some purpose, and the things you've gone through have not been in vain.

If you're struggling with questions of identity, with who you are and where life is going, start with this amazing fact: you were created for a beautiful, amazing, intentional outcome, and you will discover it!

When you think of your life this way—when you think of *yourself* this way—you'll be able to move beyond the hurts you've experienced. You can release the heavy load for something lighter.

And when you start to wonder exactly why you are here and where you are headed, remember that you are, to quote William Shakespeare, "O wonderful, wonderful, and most wonderful wonderful! And yet again wonderful, and after that, out of all hooping!"

I praise you because I am fearfully and wonderfully made;
your works are wonderful, I know that full well.
(Psalm 139:14)

Cat Memes Won't Save You

Acceptance of who you are today and where you are currently doesn't mean taking a fatalistic attitude toward life. Letting go doesn't mean giving up and just thinking the worst about your life (and everyone else's). It's easy to get down about things when you watch the news or spend any time scrolling through your social media feeds.

Unless you've blocked all the bad news and only see pictures of puppies or cat memes. Seriously, that's practically the only way to "enjoy" your daily scroll through the world of Facebook or Instagram. Just follow things that make you laugh or speak to your hobbies, because your friends are weird, their lives are a hot mess, and you are tired of "liking" photos of their kids.

If you are one of those people who pay attention to the news or politics, you are probably struggling to stay positive. I can't even watch the news because it just irritates me.

Every morning, my wife starts her day with coffee and the news, and when I come downstairs to get my own wake-up juice, I have to purposefully choose *not* to listen to what the newscasters are saying. It just frustrates me, so I have to not pay attention.

You aren't surprised.

If you've lived to at least ten years old, you've come to realize that the world is messed up. One bad moment on the playground and you know this.

The writer of Ecclesiastes knew this. *"History merely repeats itself. It has all been done before. Nothing under the sun is truly new. Sometimes people say, 'Here is something new!' But actually, it is old; nothing is ever truly new."* *(Ecclesiastes 1:9-10, NLT)*

When even a book of the Bible begins this way, it's no wonder we get discouraged. If everything just repeats itself, then it can never get better, can it? Why bother with people or the world at all? The older you get, the more you think that it's better just to stay away from it all and just isolate yourself and avoid people.

And then you become that person who scrolls through their social media and forces the rest of us to look at the cat memes. They are funny at first, sure.

But eventually, we are all going to unfollow you and not want to look at what you're posting—and then you'll start feeling even more isolated and alone (which is the danger of social media, anyway).

And then, when you've lost your internet friends, you'll be forced to actually think about how you *truly* feel about things. How you honestly feel about life, people, relationships, and all the rest.

And if you're feeling fatalistic and down about everything, you'll be convinced that life is messy, people are messy, and relationships are literally the *worst*.

After all, you know the world is messed up.

The people who run the world are messed up.

And the relationships you have are kinda messed up, too.

(See Ecclesiastes 1.)

When you decide to be fatalistic and decide that the world isn't worth it, you establish a set of rules. These rules ensure you won't get hurt, you'll avoid messy things, and you won't ever have to feel badly about others or yourself ever again. The only trouble with a rule is that there is *always* an exception to the rule.

You've decided that life is too messy? What happens when life is amazing? Like when you visit a National Park and see such beauty it actually makes your heart hurt a little bit. What happens when life is wonderful? Like when you see your daughter take off the training wheels and experience newfound freedom.

You are convinced that people are messy?

What about all the people who *aren't* on the news each day because they are doing everyday normal things like working, and trying hard to be kind, and treating others with respect?

There's a lot of them out there—which means a lot of people are actually pretty fantastic.

And relationships?

Yes, I will be honest.

They are hard.

They take work, and they can be awfully messy.

But I can't imagine my life without every relationship I've had (even the ones that are over). Life without friends I can text before a job interview knowing they will give me the encouragement I need? No, thank you. Life without family who drive me crazy but who are always there when I need them? Nope.

You see?

The world can be wonderful *and* messy.

People can be messy *and* fantastic.

And relationships will be messily wonderful.

(I just made that up.)

That's the weirdly awesome thing about our lives. The reality is that any moment, you can go from feeling elated to deflated, and you don't know when either is going to happen.

Like I said earlier, some people may wish to hunker down, isolate themselves, and just give up. (Like me, the summer between 7th and 8th grade, when I sat in my room with the blinds closed and listened to sad music and wrote plays about sad people. It was a dark time, and we will not speak of it again.)

But that will not help you move on into better things.

Accepting who you are today doesn't mean you have to kiss the future goodbye and have no hopes for what is still to come for you. In fact, acceptance is just the opposite.

It is living with a deep trust in God's wisdom and providence, knowing that He is working to do far more to make your hopes and dreams come true than anything you can do.

The world *is* a mess, and even puppy photos and cat memes can't make it go away. (Nor will reposting or sharing everything you read politically or spiritually or anything else. You can't make the mess go away by using something as messy as the internet.)

But here's a challenge for you today: instead of looking at the mess, look at the message God has for you.

The writer of Ecclesiastes may have started his book looking at the futility of everything and how the world will just keep repeating the same horribly dumb mistakes over and over again (he calls this "meaningless" which means that nothing has meaning. Does that make sense?) But he doesn't stay there.

"Yet God has made everything beautiful for its own time. He has planted eternity in the human heart, but even so, people cannot see the whole scope of God's work from beginning to end." (Ecclesiastes 3:11, NLT)

He doesn't say God has made a few things beautiful. He says *everything* is made beautiful in the time that is given to it. You don't have to spend your day sharing funny cat videos or escaping from the world. You may not see the scope of what God is up to, but you can trust that He has never stopped working.

Look at the people in your world, the relationships you have, and the incredible world you live in.

That is one way He speaks to you.

You may want to say, "Meaningless! Everything is meaningless!" like the ancient author. (I wouldn't do this. People will look at you weird.)

Instead, listen closely to what God is saying, "Don't give up, because I have never stopped working out my good plans for you."

He is able to immeasurably more than all we ask or imagine, according to His power that is at work within us.
(Ephesians 3:20)

What Are You Looking At?

A key to living a life of acceptance is *focus*.

What do you spend your time thinking about most often? If you're looking back at the times you've failed, at the hurts you've experienced, or the opportunities you missed, you'll never find joy in today. If I had a dollar for every hour I wasted I thinking back on the ways I've hurt my wife and kids, or the ways others have hurt me, or the time I didn't take the chance to speak to that person who could have advanced my career, or the weight I didn't lose—I'd be a very wealthy man and could retire on the income.

(But I'd also clearly be sad, overweight, hurtful and career-less.)

Would you want to live with a guy who made all his money from wallowing in his misery?

I asked Robyn this very question one day and she said, "How much money are we talking?"

I think she was joking, because she honestly has spent the last twenty years reminding me to stop focusing on the wrong thing. I'm not kidding about this. It happened earlier today, when I was having one of those moments she blames on me being "creative." As an artistic type, I tend to view everything as extreme peaks and valleys. There is no middle ground.

Everything in my life is either THE. WORST. THING. EVER. or it's *THE BEST!!!!*

What it comes down to isn't actually my temperament. I wish I could blame this lack of acceptance on artistic and therefore angsty and melancholy, because out of it I might actually be able to write that great novel I've dreamed of writing. (I have a couple "not great, but not bad" novels I'm working on, but they don't have that angst the *really great* novels seem to have.) But I can't blame it on my personality type.

It all comes down to focus—what I give my attention to.

For example, when I focus on not having a certain amount in the checking account, Robyn reminds me that the bills have all been paid. When I focus on our kids and their quirks and worry that maybe they will be socially awkward as adults, she reminds me that every truly remarkable person in world history was a quirky kid.

You see what I mean?

Focus is important, because it determines what we feel or think about a certain situation. While most people tend to view me as a positive person, I have a dark streak that tends to focus on the wrong thing.

Truthfully and transparently, I can tell you that it's easy to fake like you're focusing on what is good and right and perfect. At least, it's easy to think you're good at it. The people who love you and know you best are looking at you with your forced smile and that weird look in your eye and they know, "He is focusing on the wrong thing. His head is not here. He is not in this moment."

It's embarrassing when your children call you out. It's even worse when a stranger writing a book calls you out, which is what I'm doing to you, my friend.

Where's your focus?

What are you looking at?

Are you looking backwards? Are you giving your attention to the hurt and pain, the failures and all your faults? Then I want to encourage you to stop today.

Make the choice to adjust your focus.

The prophet Isaiah wrote about the importance of focus.

"You will keep in perfect peace all who trust in you, all whose thoughts are fixed on you!" (Isaiah 26:3, NLT)

Focus is where your thoughts are fixed.

What do you think about most? Where does your mind spend most of its time? You won't be able to live in peace with yourself or others when your mind is fixed on the wrong things.

Imagine your focus is like your house.

You've got a living room (or family room, or a so-called 'great room' which is just another way of saying 'we gave you less house for your money') and a garage.

One room is meant to actually *live* in. You hang out with family there, you watch movies there, you eat there when you wife is at work. You have furniture you can sit on in there. Your friends sit in there with you—it's where you laugh and talk about life and what' s going on. It's a place to *be*.

You may be one of those people who have spotless garages, and for that I applaud you. My father would be proud of you. But if you're like me, your garage is one of those places that seem to accumulate boxes. And the boxes seem to make their own boxes. And there are shelves overflowing with things and you clean it out every two or three months and pride yourself on the fact that you've left *just enough* room to squeeze the van inside.

The garage is meant to hold stuff, not to live in.

Your mind shouldn't be fixed on the past or the things that trouble or worry you. You aren't meant to live in that space, any more than you're meant to live in your garage. Fix your mind on where you are today, the good things in your life in this moment, and you'll be surprised at how much more peace you'll have in your life.

Or maybe you won't be surprised, because it's right there in that promise from Isaiah. Fix your mind on the right things, God says, and you'll find *perfect peace*.

Sometimes you'll need to go get something from the garage. That's okay. It's okay to look back once in a while. You can celebrate the things you did well and take pride in your accomplishments. It's perfectly acceptable to dust off the trophies and remind yourself, "Wow, I did good!"

But once you've looked through the boxes in your garage of memories, get back into the house. Get into the living room and reset your focus on what the Bible calls things that are *"true, and honorable, and right, and pure, and lovely, and admirable." (Philippians 4:8, NLT)*

When you struggle with thoughts of regret or worry, remind yourself that you've just taken up refuge in the garage. As clean as it may be, it's not where you're meant to stay. It's fine for the Christmas decorations and the freezer and the sleeping bags, but it's not meant for you.

Adjust your focus, my friend.

Remember, all the good things you've done, along with all the troubles you've gone through, have served one incredible purpose: to shape who you are and who are you becoming! God uses both the good and the bad to help us move beyond what was and into what will be.

Yes, your past has some bad moments in them, and you may have a few things to regret. I get it. But the next time you're tempted to take them out of the box and start looking at them, stop.

When your attention shifts from what is good to what is negative, from what is "true, and honorable and right" to something different, pause.

Pause and remember.

God's gift of perfect peace is for you, too. No matter what has happened in your past, no matter how deep your hurt. No matter your worry or stress or fear.

His perfect peace is yours.

You just need to adjust your focus.

Fix your thoughts and heart and mind on that amazing fact.

> *Rejoice in the Lord always. I will say it again: Rejoice!*
> *(Philippians 4:4)*

When You Bleed All Over Disneyland

Life is filled with good and bad, sometimes at the same time.

When you look back at the things you've posted or experienced over the years, you can easily see how quickly a day can change from one of elation to one of distress.

You know the days I'm talking about.

It starts off with everything being great. You wake up and the day is beautiful, your wife is beautiful, your kids are beautiful and you look pretty good. You go to work and everything there is beautiful, too. Your boss sings your praises in the team meeting, there's free lunch in the breakroom, and you are owning every email, message, and project. It's a great day.

But then you get that phone call.

Or you receive that text message.

Or your boss' boss knocks on your door and says, "We need to talk."

Life isn't quite so beautiful anymore. The elation deflates, the heart sinks, the emotions kick in, and now everything is ugly and dreadful, and you doubt every decision you've made since getting out of bed.

Those days.

My family had one of those days at Disneyland once.

We are a bit of a Disney family.

This is important to know as we journey through this book together, because there are going to be references to our Disney experiences here and there. My wife and I met while working at the Disney Store. We were married at Disneyland.

We frequently go to Disneyland because it's only an 18-hour drive from where we live in Seattle. (18 hours straight through, with minimal stopping, and with six people it's less expensive than flying. If you want to try it, we can give you all the pointers, tell you the best places to get gas and which rest stops to avoid.)

Anyway, we had one of *those* days at Disneyland.

Disneyland, of all places.

It was a beautiful late October day, right before Halloween. We started the magic morning with attractions, fun, music and laughter. We'd hit all the big attractions in *Cars Land* and headed into the old *A Bug's Land* to enjoy some of the more kid-friendly attractions at California Adventure.

The bumper cars were a big hit with everyone, but as we exited, August slipped on wet pavement. And by slipped, I mean fell hard, chin first.

It looked like a pretty bad scrape at first, but it was bleeding a lot and he was crying and Robyn was doing her best to keep him calm until the Disneyland nurse arrived.

She took one look at his chin and said, "He's going to have to go the emergency room."

This wasn't going to be a "quick bandage and then back to the fun" moment. We took off our Mouse ears and headed to the Orange County Children's Hospital. I waited until the doctor came in, then I watched from the door.

(My wife and I had an agreement years ago: I'll do vomit, she can do blood. It's worked out pretty good for her, since God decided to bless us with kids who barf. A lot.)

August came out fifteen minutes later with nine stitches—three of which were inside—and a giant bandage on his chin. From happiness to worry to pain to relief in the matter of an hour or so.

How we respond in moments like this shows the state of our heart.

We could have gone back to the hotel room and felt badly. We could have sat there and mourned the loss of our morning, the stitches on his chin, the pain he'd gone through. We could have sat in the hotel room, looking out at California Adventure and just watched people having fun and enjoying themselves, while feeling sad about missing out on it. But that didn't happen because he wanted to go back to Disneyland. Once we finished at the hospital, he was ready to ride the Matterhorn!

In that moment, the state of his heart modelled something for all of us: we can dwell in the pain or accept that it happens and move back into happiness. (Kids do this better than adults, so maybe God is trying to tell us something when He says the kingdom of heaven belongs to people who live like children.)

The rest of the trip, he had that bandage on his chin.

Because it was Halloween, the kids dressed up for the day and we went into the Park. It didn't slow him down, and one of my favorite pictures from the trip is him running through Fantasyland with a giant bandage on his chin. He looks every bit the pirate, with a cutlass in one hand, a tricorner hat with skull and crossbones on it, and a giant bandage on his chin. When we went on *Pirates of the Caribbean,* he looked like he belonged there. When we got home, the bandage finally came off, the stitches came out, and he was left with a small scar to forever remind him of that day.

He won't forget the wound (and neither will we, because we always point to the place he fell whenever we are at Disneyland—we are cool that way, reminding our kids when they got hurt. "Hey, Gus, remember when you fell down here and bled all over the place? Man, that was gross!"). But he also won't forget the fun and memories he had, because he chose to move beyond the wound and back into the magic.

Acceptance means you realize that God is at work in both the sun and the rain. It takes both to turn a seed into a flower, to make the grass grow, to bring renewal after the dark days of winter.

Whatever happens today, remember that He is still at work. The grey clouds of sorrow can give way to the sunshine of laughter.

Many of David's songs are like this. When you read the book of Psalms, you see that David was like a kid who cut his chin open at Disneyland. He starts one of the Psalms with a big expression of how awesome God is, but then he remembers he's being hunted all over Israel by King Saul and his mood quickly changes.

Psalm 9 begins with "I will praise you, O Lord!" and in just two verses becomes "My enemies staggered and died!" In fact, that's how the entire Psalm progresses. Praise, anger, and back to praise.

David's many songs are relatable because they remind us that whatever happens, God is still at work. He may be hounded like a criminal, unfairly treated by the king, but David still knows that God is in control. He knows that in the midst of his worst moments, God is busy at work. So in spite of the pain, he can praise.

Like the kid who cut his chin open and bled all over the "Happiest Place on Earth," you too can find a way to keep going. After the stitches, put the Mouse ears back on and take the ride on the Matterhorn.

After the pain, sing praise. Your soul will be grateful you did.

When times are good, be happy, but when times are bad consider:
God has made one as well as the other.
(Ecclesiastes 7:14)

The Tip of the Iceberg

Sometimes we struggle with acceptance because of things in our past. Hurts are going to happen, and wounds are part of life. I still remember being called short by kids in 6th grade. Just to be clear, I was and remain short. This was not news to me, but I certainly didn't enjoy being reminded of it.

I can easily recall when some kids at a new church we were visiting deliberately called me "Danielle" instead of my name. (Duane is a horrible name to grow up with—sorry, Mom and Dad—and if you're reading this and thinking about it for a future child, I implore you *don't do it!*)

As a result, I hid a book in my clothes and then hid in the bathroom at church for the next two years. I didn't want to be around people who were cruel, especially when I was short kid with a funny name.

I don't sit in my bedroom and think about it (very much) anymore, but I know how it feels to be hurt. Hurts don't just disappear. But how we *respond* to the hurt is the key to accepting who you are, today.

When we nurse the slights and hurts done to us by others, we never let them get better or heal properly. We think we are healing, but we are actually doing just the opposite. Dwelling on the pain, recreating it in our minds, living in the anger and raw emotion of the hurt just keeps the wound open. It's like having a cut that has begun to heal and then getting a knife and reopening the wound. The pain is awful, but you like talking about it, the attention you get from it. The trouble is that the wound will never get better. It will only get infected, festering, and cause you greater damage than it ever should have.

This is bitterness. Bitterness is an awful, messy thing. It keeps you focused on the hurt, not on the healing. It keeps you centered on the pain, not on the promise of the better thing that is to come. God is busy at work, but you can't see it because you're too busy looking at the wound and reminding yourself how it happened.

A great example of this is an iceberg.

(If you just started singing an old Celine Dion song, I'll wait until you are done.)

The only part of the iceberg that's visible from the surface is the smallest part. 90% of the iceberg is below the surface!

The wound and hurt that you're nursing along is like the tip of the iceberg. We focus on the tiny 10% of our lives while God (and your family and anyone who loves you) is saying,

"Hey! What about the other 90%? Look at everything else in your life!"

I know—an iceberg tends to be a negative thing thanks to a certain ship's tragic fate. But the imagery—something small is all that is visible from the surface, while the hugest part of it is hidden where we can't see it—is appropriate.

The wound in your life, the hurt and pain, is only the smallest part of your life, but that's all you can see.

In our humanity, we can't focus on the bigger picture.

We get too busy thinking of the ones who did this to us—even though they probably stopped thinking about us long ago. (Sadly, I can still remember by name the kid who was the biggest bully to me in elementary school, but I'd be surprised if he remembered mine at all. See what holding a grudge will do?)

It's ok to be wounded.

It's ok to be hurt.

Acceptance looks at those wounds and hurts and says, "It happened and yes, it sucks—*but it doesn't define me*. The wound is not who I am."

If you're struggling with this, let me give you this bit of encouragement from the apostle Paul. You may remember, he experienced a lot of wounds after he encountered Christ on the road to Damascus.

In the book of 2 Corinthians, he writes:

That's why we are not discouraged. No, even if outwardly we are wearing out, inwardly we are being renewed each and every day. This light, temporary nature of our suffering is producing for us an everlasting weight of glory, far beyond any comparison, because we do not look for things that can be seen but for things that cannot be seen. For things that can be seen are temporary, but things that cannot be seen are eternal. (2 Corinthians 4:16-18, NIV)

Paul reminds you and I that we don't need to be discouraged or give in to the temptation to be bitter. Where we can't see it, God is doing something incredible and wonderful, and that wound that is causing you so much pain and heartache today? He is busy at work doing what only He can do.

One day you will look down and see that it has healed. I grew several inches between 6th grade and high school, but I didn't notice at first, because it was gradual. I didn't suddenly shoot up, but I grew enough that someone calling me "short" no longer hurt me.

When you cut your hand, eventually the wound turns into a scar. I know this because this last year I managed to slice my hand open while putting a hinge on a door. While I was chiseling out where the hinge goes, my hand slipped, and I put a huge gash from my thumb to the middle of the back of my hand.

At first, I thought it was a minor cut.

And then I realized I could see the inside of my hand.

Blood was dripping everywhere, and it was truly ghastly.

Quickly, Robyn covered it in a towel and rushed me to urgent care. I was seeing spots, freaking out. Remember, I'm not the "blood guy" in the family, and this much blood coming out of my hand was not something I was prepared for.

But honestly—*I could see inside my hand.*

That kind of view messes a person up!

Luckily the cut wasn't deep enough to do any major damage, and the doctor determined stitches would take care of the wound. So, at nearly 50 years old, I finally received my first stitches. My hand looked like Frankenstein's monster for awhile. It hurt and ached, and it was easily one of the most physically painful things I've ever experienced. But that part is over.

It may not be exactly pretty, but the wound is gone.

It's been replaced by a reminder.

Scars are reminders that you can move on, that you were created to heal. That's what God is trying to do to the wounds of your past, too. The scar will always be there, but in time even it will fade.

Remember, God is at work, doing His healing and working His way in the wounds and hurts of your life. You may not see it happening. You may not even realize He is doing it. But when we allow Him to work out His good and perfect plan for us, the wounds and hurts and pain *will* heal. As Paul says, they are "light and temporary."

Don't give in to bitterness.

Resist the temptation to remain angry at the pain.

Refuse to reopen the wound.

Because inwardly, you are being renewed day by day.

And eventually you will look around and realize what's been happening on the inside is now visible on the outside. And it's better and more wonderful than anything you could have thought possible while you were busy focusing on the wound.

Or, as Paul says, "Far beyond any comparison." Which means it's pretty darn awesome.

Forgetting what is behind and straining toward what is ahead,
I press on toward the goal.
(Philippians 4:13b-14a)

You Don't Have to "Like" This

The word "like" hasn't had this much power in our lives since most of us were in elementary school and told someone, "I *like* her." (Or him.)

With the rise of social media, the word *like* is powerful, and a thumbs up, heart or whatever other icon currently indicates approval online can make our day or ruin it.

Thanks to places like Facebook, Instagram, Twitter, Snapchat, or whatever else has been invented since I wrote this, we now live in a world where how we feel about ourselves can be determined by the number of likes or retweets or followers you have. Social media has created an insatiable need to post and see if people give you approval.

I posted something this morning—about acceptance, actually—and I've had to resist the temptation to open my browser and see if the response has been better than I expected. I'm kind of sad that way.

You look at your friends list and take some comfort if the number is big enough—or the opposite if it's getting smaller. You enjoy the comments and really like it when you get a "love" and not just a "like." And then you kind of wonder what it means when you post something kind of personal and deep and a friend chooses the "laughter" emoji. (Either it was an accident, or they have a truly bizarre sense of humor.)

But all of that posting and sharing and tweeting and really doesn't confirm anything about you or who you are. When you share your heart in a post and get ten likes, and then share a picture of a funny looking dog and get 200 likes, you may think your worth or value are on the line.

Hard truth: it only confirms that social media is no place to go if you're having trouble with acceptance. There are several ways people use their social media accounts, and the main two are just as bad at helping you deal with letting go of the past and being okay with yourself today.

The two types of posters?

The happy family posters. You know, the ones who only ever post pictures of smiling kids, good-looking moments, and all the wonderful things in life. This used to be only visible at Christmas time, in the annual holiday card and letter.

With social media, it's our everyday lives. So we see these happy beautiful families and think: "My family isn't happy. I'm not that beautiful. What's wrong with us? We literally all spent the day yelling at each other!"

Remember: it's all just an image.

A face presented to the world. The happiest family in your feed is 100% human, imperfect, and sometimes very very messy. They fight. They argue. They don't all get along, and it may have taken several photos and a few filters to get that perfect glow on everyone's faces. And the perfect posts are their way to get some sense of validation for who they are and the choices their family makes.

The other posters, the ones who only ever post all the struggles and worries and fears? They are also looking for validation. They want people to commiserate with them, feel their pain, and tell them "It's going to be okay! You got this!" It's just the opposite side of the coin from the "happy family," and it leads to the same thing: comparison, stress, worry, and more need for responses.

Neither one is inherently bad or wrong. But it just shows that the posts and pictures and things you see are just a reflection of a moment. They are just a single moment in a lifetime of moments, and they don't reflect a life's reality.

Next time you feel temped to post—whether or happy or sad, but because you feel the need to get some validation, skip social media. Get away from your phone or your computer.

Sit down and list, on a piece of actual paper with an actual pen or pencil, all the people who really do believe in you and are rooting for you. The length of the list will probably surprise you. These names represent people who actually, in reality, truly and out of their own choice, *like* you. In reality, you have far more *likes* from real-life people than you will ever get from your friends list on social media.

Good news, though, if you're worried.

Even if your actual, real "likes" are short, there is one truly awesome thing you can count on, and it's one of the keys to letting go and living a life of acceptance.

There *is* someone who has your best interest at heart.

And if you need validation, He is no further than a prayer away.

God's love and mercy do not stop working because you are having a bad day. His providence doesn't disappear because circumstances are tricky, and His love never ends, even when the love of others has long become a memory. At the center of everything is a God who truly does love you, care for you, and is working out His plan for you, even in the middle of your worst situation.

You may feel abandoned and alone at times.

It might not feel as if He is there.

You may wish He would break the silence and give you a like or a retweet for your feelings or emotions or the things you are sharing.

(It's not going to happen. *Spoiler alert*: All the social media accounts for God are fake.)

You may not see Him working.

You may not sense His presence today.

That's *okay*, my friend.

Accept that your approval doesn't come from your posts or tweets. Don't expect to get what you are looking for from others, look to Him. He declared long ago that He loves you and cares for you. He liked you enough to create you and set you on this path.

After all, who are you living your life for? What are you doing the things you do for? The approval of a bunch of casual friends on the internet—maybe people you don't even know—or are you living your life for Him?

"Whatever you do, work at it with all your heart, as working for the Lord," writes Paul in Colossians 3:23 (NLT). Or, to say it another way: "Do your best and live your life and do *whatever you do* not to get likes or followers, but to give the *best of your heart* to the One who created you."

You don't have to like this. You just have to trust Him and remember that He is at work, directing your steps to exactly who you are becoming.

Trust in the Lord with all your heart and lean not on your own understanding;
in all your ways acknowledge Him, and He will make your paths straight.
(Psalm 3:5-6)

You are Okay

It's easier to move on into the next thing in your life when you realize that you're actually okay.

The operative word here is "okay."

It doesn't have to be perfect, wonderful, idyllic, or any other word we use to mean "better than average."

It's ok if your life is just *okay*.

Part of the trouble we have with acceptance is being okay with *okay*, because when we say "Okay" about something, we aren't saying "Yes! This is the *best*! This is *definitely* the outcome we wanted!" *Okay* means we have settled.

We think we have to have something better to move on, especially if what we had before was pretty good or even great. I've moved on from four different careers in my life, and it was only easy once: the first time. I was young, fresh out of college, not loving my first real job.

I had the impressive title of Assistant Director at an alternative learning center. In reality, I was a glorified administrative assistant who helped kids struggling with school. I liked talking through *Hamlet* with high schoolers, but the owner's husband was kind of a jerk, and when I wasn't teaching high schoolers, I was helping kindergarteners with phonics. I quickly realized I wasn't cut out for tutoring little children who needed phonics help. (When I started making faces behind their backs, I knew it was time to move on.)

It wasn't what I wanted, so moving on into the new thing was great! The new thing was magical and wonderful and everyone liked me, and I did great there because it was something I loved. (This magical place that became my next career? It starts with *D* and rhymes with "*isney.*") In fact, at that place, I met my wife. I learned a lot about leadership and creating and telling stories and a lot of things that have become part of what I do today.

But after that? After those transitions, it's kinda sucked.

Honestly, they've been hard.

One I had to move on from because of my own mistakes, another because my contract was up and there wasn't a full-time position available for me. The last one I had to move on from because people in authority made decisions that made it clear it was time to move on.

Were they ideal transitions?

Nope.

Was what I moved into perfect and exactly what I wanted?

Not at all.

I went from a huge office leading a big team of people with events and audiences of thousands to a workspace in the corner of my living room and a cat that won't stay off my keyboard.

(I'm not joking. He likes it, but I find it a bit annoying.)

But acceptance reminds me that I'm not trying to move into the best place God has for me today, because I might not be ready for it. Maybe He's trying to teach me something first to get me ready. Maybe He's doing the same thing for you, too.

It might be kind of like how you need to work extra hard to get ready for those vacations where swimsuits are involved.

God also might surprise you.

You may wake up one morning and realize when you look around at where you today, He is saying, *"THIS IS THE PLACE. You're already here!"* And you'll know it because you'll feel that incredible sense of relief and joy and promise and look back and wonder how you missed it.

Isaiah 43:18-19 reminds us of this.

God's people are wondering if where they are is where they will always be. Yes, they've messed up a lot and some of their current circumstances are a result of their own decisions and folly. But God doesn't abandon them anymore than He's going to abandon you. He says, "Forget all that! Your past is *peanuts* compared to what is coming next! I'm going to do something so amazing and new it will blow your mind! Seriously—*look around and see what I am up to!*"

That is my rather loose interpretation.

The New Living Translation puts it this way: "*But forget all that—it is nothing compared to what I am going to do. For I am about to do something new! See, I have already begun! Do you not see it?*" (Isaiah 43:18-19a)

They missed it for the same reason we miss it. Because humans tend to be kind of short-sighted.

When we are so busy looking for what is next, we're missing the huge opportunity right in front of us. If I spend all my time wondering what might happen if I do *this*, and God is saying, "Hey, dummy, just do *this*!" then I'm not living with acceptance either.

It's okay to be just "ok."

Stay in that place for a while.

You may get back on top, you may get moved to a new mountain altogether, you may stay right where you are. God has a plan and a purpose for you—but you may never see it if you expect perfection to show up right now, in this moment. What He may want for you is to accept that you are fine where He has put you today and do the best you can right there.

He's already begun doing a new thing, even if you can't see it. So say to yourself, "Hey—it's okay."

The Lord will keep you from all harm—He will watch over your life.
(Psalm 121:7)

Life is a Highway

Surprise!

Your life is not done!

Let that sink in a minute, especially if you've been hurt recently or lost something dear to you. Your identity may be wrapped up in that thing. Your reason for getting out of bed in the morning may be what you just lost. You had some nasty, horrible things happen to you.

But your life is not over.

Your journey is still going. And journeys have a way of taking you places you may never expect. I've discovered this over many years of taking road trips with my family.

We've been doing long ones—several thousand miles a stretch—for over a decade. We've traveled across the entire western half of the United States on some really crazy small roads. We've seen towns that forgot they existed and driven down some roads that didn't even deserve the term.

We spent a good portion of one trip on a dirt road in Wyoming. It was miles and miles of rocks and dirt and endless reminders that this was not optimal minivan terrain. *This is not a location featured in the Honda commercials.* This is where you realize how incredible my wife is, because she didn't just divorce me as soon as we hit the actual highway again.

When you take a road trip, you accept that getting there is part of the fun. What you see along the way is part of the experience. You don't take a road trip with the purpose of getting somewhere quickly, especially in Montana.

Life is like a road trip.

It's a journey.

Some might even say that "life is a highway" and you're gonna drive it "all night long." (Great song, and the Rascal Flats version from the movie *Cars* is definitely on any road trip playlist. For another great road trip song, check out "I Love This Drive," from the *Cars*-themed album, "Mater's Car Tunes." Yes, it's another Disney song, but it's how every road trip playlist starts for us.)

You may be a little tired of the "life is a highway" metaphor. And it's true, it's been used a lot. But bear with me—if you're driving somewhere and get a flat tire, do you repair the flat? Or do you just say, "We're done. We live here now?"

We've had car trouble on our trips—one time the windshield wipers refused to turn off on a drive through Oregon—but we didn't say, "Ok, kids. Sorry, we're done with our trip. No Disneyland for you. Bad windshield wipers, you know."

Another time, we got a flat tire driving down the side of a mountain. We didn't turn to each other and say, "Welcome to our new home, here at the intersection of broken-down Honda and wherever the heck we are."

In both instances, we found a way to get repairs and continue the trip. Sometimes it's clear what needs to be done. When the tire blew as we drove into the San Fernando Valley, we had to pull over on the busy interchange of what I'm pretty sure is four hundred California freeways, take the luggage out of the trunk, and get out the spare.

We had the help of a very nice California Highway Patrol officer who took pity on us—he saw the little kids in the back seat of the Honda and made sure nobody hit me as I put the spare tire on. He directed us to a nearby tire shop, we replaced the flat tire, got back in the car, and eventually ended up at Disneyland.

Sometimes it's not so clear.

The faulty windshield wiper had a short, and the part was nowhere in town, meaning several days of waiting. We learned how to wiggle the handle enough to turn it off and headed down the road. This was awkward on the road trip, but when we got home to Seattle, where it *always rains*, we became experts.

The point is, don't give up.

A verse I first learned in third grade seems appropriate here. The journey you are on—the path you are taking—you're not doing it alone. So, take inspiration from a song David wrote about traveling.

In Psalm 121, he—and a bunch of other pilgrims on the road to Jerusalem—see the sights around them and are amazed.

Like driving down the California coast and seeing Big Sur or crossing the Continental Divide in the middle of the Rocky Mountains, there are incredible views along the journey. David says, "Look at those mountains! Aren't they amazing? But if trouble comes, will the mountains help me? No way. My help comes from the One who *made* the mountains!"

God knows the journey won't be easy.

He knows you'll need to stop for repairs along the way.

And He wants to remind you that not only will He be there to help you when you need it, He's doing something pretty cool. He's watching over your entire journey, from start to finish—which means you *will* get there in one piece.

"The Lord keeps watch over you as you come and go, both now and forever." (Psalm 121:8, NLT)

Knowing that, it should change the way you view those moments along the road when bad things happen and cause you to lose your momentum.

Instead of giving up, look at where you are as a repair that needs to be done. If you're feeling flat, what can you do to lift yourself up? If you're feeling run down, how can you jump start your spirit? When you view everything as a journey, you realize that the places you've passed through and the people you've met are just part of the adventure and you're not even close to reaching your destination.

In other words, your life isn't over.

The trip is just getting started and you have a long way to go.

Stop for necessary repairs, use the bathroom, and do whatever else you need to do along the road. Stop and see the sights, make some memories.

But don't stop *stop*.

Don't quit altogether.

You're not alone on this road, and your help doesn't come from AAA. It comes from the One who created the road—the One who made the sights you're seeing—and promises to get you there safely, no matter what happens or whatever troubles come your way. So, no matter where you find yourself, don't give up.

Accept that some places on the journey are better than others and keep moving.

But in keeping with His promise, we are looking forward a new heaven
and a new earth, the home of righteousness.
(1 Peter 3:13)

Snow Days

Let go of the problems you face today.

You may not be able to change your circumstance, but you can change your response to it. It's like my wife and I always say to our kids: "Choose your response."

A classic way to look at this is when snow falls.

I live in Seattle, so we don't get a lot of big snow days. Maybe one or two big snows a year, and the rest are light dustings. But because of all the hills everywhere, and the lack of frequent snowfall, people here tend to view any appearance of a snowflake as the END OF DAYS. Even a hint of snow in the forecast and one local news station treats it like SNOWPACALYPSE, with constant fretful updates and brave newscasters standing on street corners interviewing the terrified populace.

The populace *is* terrified.

There's a gut response to the words "Chance of snow," and it's not a pretty one. Tension, worry, fear, and flat out terror. These are many people's response to that terrible four-letter word. (S-N-O-W.)

They refuse to drive—or forget how to drive altogether—and every grocery store aisle is filled with terror-stricken adults fighting over coffee (it's Seattle, after all) and toilet paper, the two necessary ingredients for survival. Gas stations get backed up or run out of gas, social media pages flood with warnings about the dangers of snow and ice. Normally sane adults freak out when the snow falls and can't sleep, worried over what the snow will bring them.

But kids?

They see it and jump for joy.

Kids see the news of school cancelations due to snow and begin thinking the words "snow day," and it's as if it's Christmas Day, their birthday, and the start of summer vacation combined.

Snow days are wonderfully crazy things.

When kids hear the words "Chance of snow," they react in a very predictable way. Just like adults, they have a gut response to those two words. They start trying to find their snow clothes, wondering how deep it will get, check on snowman supplies and ask if there's enough hot cocoa. If the forecast changes from chance to "it's happening," they fall asleep with the blinds open and watch the streetlights to see the first falling snowflakes.

So, while their parents watch the late-night news with trepidation, kids fall asleep with nothing but excitement for the possibilities the next day's snowfall will bring them.

Same circumstance, two completely different responses.

This is why life is like a snow day.

When we find ourselves in a place we didn't expect or want to be, how do we respond? Usually, our humanity comes out and we react like adults on a snow day.

It's END OF DAYS.

It's the end of all good things and we are *definitely* not going to make it! We lay in bed, thinking about what might happen tomorrow, and think of how woefully unprepared we are. We begin to worry and stress out.

A new place or an unexpected chance of something we didn't plan on is not what God wants for you or me. That's not what He intends when He allows something new and different in our lives.

Remember that verse where God promises He is doing a new thing? That *new thing* may be something you don't expect. It may be something unfamiliar that causes a bit of extra work for you. An extra bit of faith or even a bit more patience.

Earlier in the same passage, the prophet shares this promise from God.

> *"When you go through deep waters,*
>   *I will be with you.*
> *When you go through rivers of difficulty,*
>   *you will not drown.*
> *When you walk through the fire of oppression,*
>   *you will not be burned up;*
>   *the flames will not consume you." (Isaiah 43:2 NLT)*

I might add "When you face a lot of snow, you will not slip on the ice and break your leg or plow into the car next to you." (Seriously, it gets so bad here in Seattle that people just abandon their cars on the road when it snows. So you need a *lot* of those promises from God to make it safely down the road.)

Whatever thing you are facing, even if it's not what you expect, God is there and this new or unknown thing is not a problem to overcome, but another chance to experience a greater trust and faith in the One who promises to be with you through all of them.

I know—it's not easy.

In our humanity, we view this new or unknown or uncertain place as an obstacle, a worry, and something we need to overcome. But maybe we should view this new place the way God wants us to. Maybe, instead of looking at this "chance of something" as terrifying and worrisome, we need to view it as a snow day.

A world covered in snow seems unfamiliar and strange. You know it's the same trees, the same street, the same patio furniture. But covered in snow? Now it looks like something full of unknown and wonderful possibilities. Instead of fearing it, we need to just see the snow like kids do.

Kids see snowflakes as opportunities, not obstacles.

That's how God wants you to view this new and unfamiliar place, too. It's not an obstacle to overcome, but an opportunity to discover something new, something wonderful, and maybe even enjoy yourself in the process.

God reminds you and I of this every time snow falls.

Let God remind you today: "I made the place you are at right now just as much as I made the last place and the one, I will bring you to next." Or, as He promised, "I am doing something new! Look—it's already begun!"

Relax and enjoy where you are.

You may miss your day at the beach, but God has sent you snowflakes. You can either see snowpacalypse or snowmen. The choice is up to you.

Let us hold unswervingly to the hope we profess, for He who promised is faithful.
(Hebrews 10:23)

Sinkholes and Potholes

Did you make a mistake in your past?

Did you screw up big time?

Congratulations, you are completely normal!

I know that may not be what you want to hear today, but it's true. Every single person in the history of this planet—save one—has a laundry list of mistakes and mess-ups and oops-I-did-it-agains.

The problem with us is that we tend to look at the mistakes and messes in our past and view them as something much larger than they actually are. In fact, rather than viewing our past troubles as what they are, we view them as sinkholes.

Sinkholes are a really crazy phenomenon. Everything looks great on the surface, but geologic forces are at work far below. Eventually, there is enough erosion that it can't support the surface ground anymore, and the entire thing gives way. One morning in 1981 this happened to a lady named Mae Rose Williams.

She heard a swishing sound and watched a 40-foot-tall sycamore tree near her home in Winter Park, Florida, disappear into a hole. Within hours, her entire house was swallowed up by the same hole, along with a city swimming pool, several Porsches, a travel trailer, and part of a city street. It was one of the largest sinkhole events in American history. It devoured everything it could until it was full, and eventually filled up with water, stabilizing itself. Today, the sinkhole is called Lake Rose in honor of the lady whose house disappeared.

We tend to look at the times we messed up in our lives as sinkholes like the one in Winter Park. We see this bad thing in our past growing ever larger and ready to devour anyone who comes close. And since we tend to stay too connected to the past, we are in constant danger of falling in. Sinkholes can mess things up for a time, and yes, things can get lost in them. But like the one that ate Mae Rose's house, they eventually stop and can become something beautiful.

Your past mistakes and screw ups are not sinkholes.

It is the rare person in the world who makes such colossal mistakes in their life that they cannot recover from them.

If your marriage fell apart, sorry, but that's not the end of the world. It happened, something went bad. But it's not a sinkhole.

Did you have a bad relationship with your kids? Not a sinkhole.

Did you mess up at work and lose your job? Not a sinkhole.

Someone did something to you and it's hard to see beyond the anger and hurt? Repeat after me: *not a sinkhole.*

It's time to view the messes of your past not as sinkholes, but potholes.

Potholes can throw you for a loop when you first drive over them, but they are pretty easy to pave over and repair. Unlike sinkholes, potholes take relatively no time to fix. Utility crews can show up, stop traffic for an hour or two, and voila! New pavement is done and the road is drivable again.

The road might not be quite as even as it was the first time you drove on it, but when you look back at it, you'll just see a slightly different color of pavement to remind you of where it used to be.

God is in the business of helping us pave over our past.

When His utility crew of Grace & Mercy show up, they clean up the pothole, get the gunk out of it, and put new pavement down. Grace says that the mess is not so big it can't be forgiven. Mercy says your mess is not going to ruin you, even though it had the potential to.

If you made a mistake or screwed up or whatever other metaphor you want to use for hurting or being hurt by someone, remember that it's not the end of the world. It's not a sinkhole. It's just a pothole, and your journey doesn't end with one pothole.

It's bumpy.

It's not fun when you hit it.

It may even cause you to stop when you didn't expect.

But grace and mercy are there, ready to do the wonderful things they do, if we let them.

The apostle Paul reminds us of this in his letter to the Philippians. He urges them to "Forget what lies behind."

Now, you and I both know it's impossible to forget the past and our mistakes and the things we've done completely. But Paul is not advocating an appearance by the Men in Black to give you a memory wipe.

Warren Wiersbe, in his commentary on the book of Philippians, suggests that Paul is encouraging us to "no longer be influenced by or affected by" the past. There's a big difference between remembering the past and being affected by it.

Paul encourages us to strain for what lies ahead instead.

Push forward, never stopping for an hour or two or "remember whens." He knows that God is busy at work, repairing the past, helping us reclaim it for God's good and glory.

Keep moving forward.

Walt Disney was a big advocate of this, too.

When people suggested he capitalize on the phenomenal success of the 1933 Silly Symphony *The Three Little Pigs* by making more cartoons with the characters, he replied, "You can't top pigs with pigs." (Which is very good advice, actually.)

Toward the end of his life, as Walt kept pushing his team beyond animated films and into thinking of ways to improve life, he said, "Around here, however, we don't look backwards for very long. We keep moving forward."

Good advice—Walt understood that looking at your failures or troubles as insurmountable would never help him achieve his goals. He was constantly in financial worry and stress, putting his personal fortune on the line time and again.

He lost tons of money along the way.

He lost friends.

He lost his faith in the studio he'd built.

But if he stayed focused there, there would have been no *Snow White*, no *Wonderful World of Disney*, and no Disneyland or Walt Disney World. Walt understood: his problems were not sinkholes. They were potholes, and they were not going to stop him from moving forward.

Whether it's Paul or Walt, the point is the same.

Stop looking at your past and start looking at your future. Sinkholes may make the national news, but potholes do not. It's hard to ignore a giant sinkhole, but nobody pays attention to potholes— because they are common, every day things.

Your past screw-up or mistake may seem overwhelming and huge to you, but in the vast history of the world and in eternity, it's not. Because everyone has a past, everyone has something they need to move forward from, *every* thing you regret or wish never happened is not a monumental problem to overcome.

Not a sinkhole.

Even better?

God uses your paved-over potholes to make the journey easier for others. What you learned and experienced in your mess can help you help others when they face similar situations. What caused a big bump on your journey turns into smooth driving for the ones coming behind you.

And if your problem seems so huge that you can't see it as anything except a sinkhole?

Remember that sinkhole that ate part of Winter Park, Florida? It's now a beautiful lake with pathways and playgrounds. People may remember the sinkhole, but that's not what they see anymore.

Take heart. Keep moving forward.

And that horrible mistake or mess you've made?

Not a sinkhole.

And we know that in all things God works for the good of those who love Him, who have been called according to His purpose.
(Romans 8:28)

Reflections

Have you ever looked in the mirror and thought, "Ugh. Who is that?"

I know, probably at least every morning, the older you get, right?

But have you ever looked and wished you *didn't* look that way?

Too short?

Too tall?

Too fit?

Not fit enough?

Spend enough time in front of a mirror and you'll find something to dislike about yourself. It's why the fashion, makeup, fitness and food industries make billions of dollars a year: because we as humans are really not very accepting of ourselves.

If you've got issues with your appearance, maybe it's time to stop and think differently about yourself.

I understand, because I've always been what most people would call for lack of a better term, *short*. (I may have mentioned this earlier.)

Throughout elementary school, there was only one brief, wonderful year where I was not the shortest boy in the class. (Thank you, Mike M., wherever you are. You helped make Third Grade amazing!)

Even now, I'm not very tall.

If my wife wears heels, she towers over me. My oldest son finally is about an inch taller than me, and when I look at my youngest son's long lanky legs, I'm certain he's going to look down on me one day. And that's a good thing.

It's okay for me to think about my height in that way.

It's okay for me to pay attention to my weight, because I want to avoid the health issues that come from being unhealthy at my height. It's okay for me to do exercises to reduce my waist line and build up my strength. It's okay for me to make healthy choices.

What is not okay is when I start looking at my reflection in the mirror and hating what I see. It's not okay if I start wishing I was different. If I look at myself and the height I am and the shape I am and think, "Nice job, God. Why didn't you make me taller? Why did you make me have the same body type as my grandfather? Why can't I look like I did when I was 21?" That's resentment and bitterness and kind of a rude way to talk to the one who made me.

When I think that way, I lose sight of something important.

God made me this way on purpose.

David reminds us of this in Psalm 139.

"Thank you for making me so wonderfully complex! Your workmanship is marvelous..." (Psalm 139:14)

You may not think of yourself as marvelous, but when you consider just how amazingly complex your body is, you have to marvel at what God did when He put the human form together. (Marvel is defined by Webster's as being "filled with wonder or astonishment." When you look at your body, *that* should be your response. Not, "Ugh.")

My height is what it is for a reason, not just because of an accident of genetics or heredity. He chose my size for a reason, and He created me with all my freckles and those weird calcium deposits in my arm and the beard that is entirely grey on my chin and nowhere else.

God made me short for a reason.

And that reason, if I truly believe it, is *marvelous.*

It *wasn't* just so I'd be the shortest kid in Mrs. Okamoto's 6th grade class. The way I was made was for something far more "wonderful and astonishing." You see, when God put me together and created me, He had a good idea of who I would be, too—and what I would eventually do someday.

I've been a teacher and a pastor and a Disney cast member—and in all of those careers, I've worked with a lot of kids. *A lot* of kids.

I think God knew that, and He made me short for that reason.

When I was a pastor, I was the same height as most of the kids in my ministry. At least the little kids. Once they hit 5th and 6th grade, they usually surpassed me.

But they could relate to me in a way they couldn't to other authority figures. They could look me in the eye, I didn't have to work to get "down to their level." As an authority figure, I didn't come across as big and scary.

Even to this day, when I share with kids or work with them, I don't have to work extra hard to see where they are coming from, because that is where I live, too.

The Bible has numerous verses where we see how each of us were created wonderfully and purposefully, by a Creator who carefully crafted us before we were born. Even better, he gives our bodies purpose as we grow up. He gives us the bodies we have, the faces we have, the noses we have, the freckles and moles and even the warts—for a reason.

I spent my whole life wishing to be taller, only to discover that the place He had for me would be better if I wasn't extra tall.

And luckily, I still tower over a few third graders.

What about you? The things you don't like about yourself—maybe it's time to start viewing them differently. Because honestly, if you can't even accept your body, you're going to miss out on some of the good things God is doing right now. You're going to miss out because you're too busy focusing on the wrong thing and doing the wrong thing to improve the way you think about the reflection in the mirror.

Get healthy.

Make sure you're taking care of the body God gave you.

But don't freak out if it's not what you think it should be. Don't overwhelm your Pinterest board with workouts and follow every fitness person on Instagram.

Or as Baz Luhrmann's hit song from the 1990's, "Everybody's Free to Wear Sunscreen," so aptly reminds us:

"Don't read beauty magazines. They will only make you feel ugly."

Look at yourself in the mirror today. Do it as soon as you're done reading this. But today, find a way to look at yourself differently. Find joy in the crazy awesome way your body looks or acts or feels.

Marvel at His creativity.

Be filled with astonishment and wonder!

Because He made *you*. And remind that reflection in the mirror that you were made for a plan and a purpose. You may not know it today, but you *will* discover it.

Accept it, warts or calcium deposits and all.

But in fact, God has arranged the parts in the body, every one of them,
just as he wanted them to be.
(1 Corinthians 12:18)

There is a Quiet Place

We live in a world that loves distractions.

Even as I write this, I see a notification from my phone, a new email has just come in, and the person sitting across from me at the coffee shop has started picking his nose.

Distractions are everywhere and come in many shapes and sizes (and nostrils and finger sizes).

How many times have you wished you could focus better? (You may just want go back and read the chapter about focus again.)

Have you wondered what life would be like with less distractions?

So many things draw our attention.

Our watches alert us, our phones buzz, our computers ding, we get messages on our televisions and game consoles. Even if you're sitting and trying to relax, the world around you is trying to remind you that it's there.

Truth is, when we are struggling with acceptance, we like those distractions, don't we? If we have too much going on in our heads—if we are worried or afraid or really don't like where we are right now—we welcome those alerts:

"Thank God! This bulk email sent from the online retailer with specials I don't really care about will stop me from thinking too much today!"

I get it.

I have two screens when I use my computer, and I always keep my email open on one of them. Every time a new email comes in, I glance over to see if *this is the good one*, but even when it's not, I still take time to stop and delete it, send it to junk mail, or just give it a glance.

So. Many. Distractions.

It may seem hard to turn them off or not give them our attention, but we can do it. The secret is in choosing to let go. Honestly—it's not just a handy place to remind you of the title of the book. Letting go is a gift that will help stop the distractions.

When we are more at peace with who and where we are—when we have learned to accept ourselves and our situation— we don't need so many things to grab our attention.

We like distractions when we are unhappy or worried or sad because they help divert our minds from the troubles we face. This is why it's easy to decide to "check on Facebook" and look up and realize an hour has gone by. If the day is bad or we are not enjoying life, what better way to not have to think about it?

There is a better way to deal with it, though.

Let go and accept your life as it is right now, today.

Accepting life as it is today means you are more okay with what you face. It means you don't need to run from it. You don't need an escape. You don't need something artificial to keep your mind from thinking too much.

This isn't new.

We may be more distracted by technology than our forebears, but humanity has always craved a distraction from what is now. Artists use creativity to distract them from their worries and stress and fear— it's usually how most of the great masterpieces of art came into existence.

Others built things while others invented. It's not necessarily bad, but the more noise we need to fill our empty spaces, to eliminate the quiet, to keep us from thinking too much about the things we worry about, the less simple our lives are.

God reminds us very often that quiet is good.

David wrote, "Be still and know that I am God."

Jesus got away from the noise and hustle of the crowd.

Elijah heard God's voice not in the storm or the wind, but in the quiet.

In fact, there are nearly 200 references to being quiet or quietness in the Bible. Whether it's being quiet and not saying anything or just resting or looking forward to a time when Jerusalem will be a "quiet habitation," there are many instances where the Bible suggests we do more to enjoy silence and quiet moments.

There is an old song my grandfather loved that says, "There is a quiet place far from the rapid pace where God can soothe my troubled mind." (The *a capella* group *Take 6* did a beautiful rendition on their debut album if you'd like to hear it.) The lyricist acknowledges that troubled minds are not places where calm and quiet reign. And the only place to soothe that trouble is in the quiet, away from the hustle and bustle of everyday life.

How many of us could use more of that these days?

(Trick question—*all* of us need more of this.)

If you found a moment to just be quiet, to rest and listen, what would God say to you? What if you were able to silence the noise, turn off the notifications and just listen? What do you think would happen?

Getting away from the noise and the distractions may be the very thing we need to be able to accept where we are right now. When we are quiet, we may find that God is speaking and what He's saying is, "It's okay. You are okay. You matter, you have value, and I went to the greatest lengths possible to remind you."

It's not easy when so much demands your attention.

Family, job, spouse, kids, friends.

But here's the crazy thing: the quieter we get, the more we enjoy it. It's true.

When we get moments to pause and just *rest*, our bodies and minds begin to want more and more of it.

We start to crave the solitude and quiet.

Then we tend to worry less about what we will tell ourselves in the quiet because we start listening for *His* voice and what *He* wants to say to us.

God knows we need solitude and quiet and rest. He created us for it, and modeled it for us, too. After the busy hectic days of creation, God hit the pause button, turned on airplane mode, and rested. It's right there in Genesis 2, verse 1: *"On the seventh day God had finished His work of creation, so he rested from all His work."* *(NLT)* All of creation was making noise—but He unplugged Himself from it. He took in the quiet.

When you're done resting, turn on the notifications, plug back in. You may discover you don't like it as much as you used to, and you'll be less likely to long for distractions. Follow the example of God Himself, and rest.

There is plenty of time to yell and shout and sing. But there is also plenty of time to just be quiet.

> *A time to be quiet, and a time to speak…*
> *(Ecclesiastes 3:7b)*

Take a Break

How often do you take a break?

And by break, I mean physically stopping the work you are doing to push away from the desk and get somewhere that work and what is required of you right now is no longer a concern.

You know, a *break*—for at least for a few minutes at a time each day.

This is one of the hardest things about letting go.

Accepting where and who we are is tough for many of us, because work is what gives us our identity. What we *do* has come to define who we *are*. We don't meet new people and ask questions that might help us understand the way they think.

When we first meet people, we tend to start with the standard question: "So," awkward pause, "what do *you* do?"

I would love to be able to ask different questions.

I would love to ask questions that would honestly help me get to know how a person thinks or feels. I personally think this would be an amazing way to live life.

Instead of asking someone, "What do you do?" the next time you meet them, ask a different question. This will startle them, because on the list of *Acceptable Questions When First Meeting Someone*, the questions lean toward the big four: "What do you do?" and "What's your name?" and "Where do you live?" and "Where are the snacks?"

Imagine at the next awkward dinner party, you walk up to someone and skip the standard questions. Instead, ask, "What's your favorite movie?" The answer to *that* question will tell you *a lot* about a person.

Our favorite movies give amazing insight into our personalities and how we view the world—and it can save time, too. You and I both know it's hard to be friends with someone who loves that many Nicolas Cage movies. (My apologies to anyone who names *The Rock* or *National Treasure* as their favorite films. But seriously. Really?)

If, when we first met, you asked, "What are your favorite movies?" and I answered with *"Pinocchio, Chariots of Fire, Schindler's List, and The Lord of the Rings* films." You'd get a good idea of what kind of person I am—and with a list like that, it may start a whole *new* group of unexpected questions.

What if we asked, "What's your favorite color?" or "How many National Parks have you visited?" Questions like these get past the surface and could so easily help us understand and get along better with everybody.

Sadly, I know this won't happen because when I try it people just look at me like I'm crazy.

So instead, we ask, "What do you do?"

If you'd asked me that two years ago, I could have answered it easily. I had a "real" job. I was "Pastor Duane." I worked for an organization who paid me to deliver a service and I had a title. When that went away unexpectedly, I was at a loss.

Until recently (and by that, I mean yesterday), I really, truly struggled with that question.

"What do you do?"

I honestly have issues with it today, because currently it's a little hard to put into words what I do. I write, I draw, I design. Sometimes I speak in public and sometimes I perform weddings. So when people ask me what I do, I have a hard time answering.

When I first left my job as a pastor, I stammered and hesitated. Without that title of "Pastor Duane," I felt like I had lost my identity and could not accept a large part of whoever this new version of me was going to be.

Many of us struggle with this. "Who" we are is defined by what we "do."

But what if we aren't doing *anything*?

Do we still have purpose and a reason for existing and all the rest?

If I'm not working—and I don't mean not having a job, I honestly mean not working. You know, actively choosing to stop and rest and get away from *work,* including access to work emails and messages on our phones. If I'm not doing *work*, do I have value?

If you're one of those people who struggle with taking a day off, or even taking a long lunch break now and then—if you're someone who can't sit and read a book or watch a favorite show or just listen to a piece of music in the backyard on a sunny day—then I implore you to stop.

It's time to get away from this idea that if we are doing something, we have an identity and a place in the world. Accept that you still have value and worth even when you aren't *doing* something.

God didn't create you to constantly be moving or working.

He didn't make us so we'd always be rushing around.

Take a break.

It's good advice.

It's also a whole song in the show *Hamilton*, and if Alexander had listened, everything would have worked out so much better for him, his family, and American history. Seriously. Go listen to the Broadway album (if you haven't already) and see how different things might have been if he'd heeded his wife's advice. It's okay to take a break—and sometimes it could change the course of history. Or at least *your* history.

There is so much more to life than being busy.

God gave you a world to explore.

People to know.

He gave you life so you could actively *live*, not just do a job and earn a paycheck. So get off your phone, get away from the computer, and go looking. Go find your thing. Find the thing that gives you your break, your rest or pause, and do it.

For some, that will be playing video games, for others, it's watching some bad television, others will enjoy a hike or a bike ride. Because we are all so wonderfully unique, nobody has the same exact ideal way of taking a break. I like to sit and just listen to my favorite Disneyland music loops. Honestly—the music that plays in the *Grizzly Peak* area of California Adventure is music that brings me peace and joy and relaxation.

Robyn loves to watch television—she enjoys the celebrity and entertainment news shows and finds them a way to wind down after a busy day at work.

But we *both* love many of the same things that help us press *pause* and take a break.

We both love just getting in the car and driving down scenic roads, away from freeways and the city. We've had some wonderfully restful moments that way. And when we were out taking our break, what we did for a living wasn't important. It didn't matter whether I was a pastor or marketing manager at large Northwest software firm. It didn't matter that she was a retail manager. Our "who-ness" was more evident in those moments than our job titles or positions would ever reveal.

When we take our breaks, we discover a bit more about who God created us to be. Job titles come and go, but the unique and wonderful creation that you are is far more wonderful and valuable. Find what brings you joy and peace and then tell people about it.

Let go of your title.

Let go of your position.

Embrace your breaks. Find worth in the things that bring you peace and joy and a bit of happiness. God created you for those things, to enjoy them and find solace in them when life gets busy or crazy.

Remember, who you are is not defined by what you *do*.

You can discover that much easier when you don't do anything at all.

A little sleep, a little slumber, a little folding of the hands to rest.
Proverbs 6:10

You Can't Fix Everyone

There is something nobody likes to talk about when it comes to letting go.

Throughout this entire book, you may have noticed that I talk a lot about you and me, and even use the pronoun "we" often. It's easy to think about what it means to let go for yourself, personally.

But acceptance isn't just about you.

You can say, "I'm letting go and I accept where I am today because I know that God has an incredible plan and purpose worked out for me."

You can say that.

And you probably have said that (maybe a bit more since you started reading this book)! But then you turn around and realize all those people who hurt you or annoy you or are sharing a house with you need to change, too.

You're not really accepting anything if you see everyone around you and think, "They need to change."

It's good to look in the mirror and start to like the person you are seeing there. It's part of God's plan and wish for you to marvel at how He made you and to trust that He is watching your travels and walking the road with you. But when you walk away from the mirror and run into that person who bugs you or annoys you and demand they get their act together the way you'd like them to, then you haven't really started living a life of acceptance.

As you come to enjoy and learn more about how good life can be right now, today, you'll become more aware of the things you like and enjoy. Maybe it's a musical style or a television show or a certain writer. Maybe you've discovered how much you love working out. Good for you—after all, God created you to enjoy things and appreciate them!

Here's where I struggle.

The world is full of annoying people who don't like the same musical style, television show, or book as you. They don't even share the same opinion as you! I know—this is difficult, and it can affect your relationships.

The first true argument Robyn and I ever had was in one of these moments. We were driving to dinner while we were dating, and the topic of our favorite movies came up.

I said that my favorite film was *Schindler's List*.

She looked at me like I was crazy and said, "That movie is so boring." I looked at her as if she had just told me she was actually an alien and wanted to remove my brain for scientific study.

All I could think was, "How could this incredibly perfect human being who has no flaws at all be so dumb when it comes to movies?"

Luckily, I didn't say it that way. But it did lead to an argument because I tried to convince her she was wrong not to love *Schindler's List* as much as I did.

To this day, we don't share the entire same list of things we enjoy. I love film music, she prefers pop music. I like crime dramas, she would rather watch a sitcom. She thinks *Star Wars* is stupid. It's okay that we don't like the same things, but I've had to learn to be okay with it. Lucky for her, I learn quickly, and it's only taken me 20 years of marriage.

Other people who aren't related to me are much more difficult to accept. Like those people at the gym who sweat, make funny noises, and like to give themselves pep talks while you're straining to reach a new goal on the chest press. (This may or may not be a personal experience.)

Acceptance reminds you that you can't change people around you.

You can't force someone to like what you like, to take comfort in the things that bring comfort to you. And you honestly can't tell someone at the gym that they should stop making annoying noises. (Remember my earlier comments about my height?)

Because if you go around telling them all the ways they need to change, they will tell you what you need to change, too. And you know what your problem areas are, so do you really want a stranger saying your nose whistles when you jog on the treadmill?

Yeah, probably not.

God made you unique and wonderful and quirky.

He did the same thing for them.

The marvelous, wonderous, astounding way He created you? Yeah, it's across the board. It's how He made *all of us.*

So, as you journey into accepting yourself, start to learn to accept others as well. Find things to appreciate about them. Find positive ways to interact with them. After all, they are probably struggling with the journey of acceptance, too.

It's why they are at the gym or blasting their music at the stoplight. They've been asking the same questions you have about who they are and where they are going. And they may just need a little encouragement to help them like who they are today.

Paul puts it this way:

"Don't look out only for your own interests, but take an interest in others, too." (Philippians 2:4, NLT)

I love how the New Living Translation says that. "Take an interest in others, too." To "take an interest" in something means to give it attention, to give it your time. When you take an interest in others, you discover the things you have in common and share and give them the gift you've been working on.

Acceptance.

It's much easier to accept someone else when you take an interest in what they do and care about. You eventually discover commonality and things you can share.

A great example in my life is *The Lord of the Rings* films.

I'd loved the books for a very long time. I never, ever in my wildest dreams would have guessed they would be Robyn's favorite films. Ever since they were released in theatres, viewing them together has been an annual event in our house.

Every year after Christmas, we get out the Extended Edition versions of both *The Hobbit* and *The Lord of the Rings* and watch them all the way through.

She loves Bilbo and Gandalf and Arwen and Legolas. She loves the moment where Gandalf stops the Balrog ("You shall not pass!") and the music that plays when the film gets to Rohan. She loves the moment when Thorin reminds us that if we all loved home and hearth more than gold "it would be a merrier world."

She may not like *Schindler's List*, but that's okay.

Acceptance helps us discover some things about others that you can like. Or appreciate. Or even just tolerate. You may discover you have far more in common than you realize. You may find that you actually have a shared love and passion.

Don't try to change them. Don't try to force them to be like you, act like you, or even think like you. Appreciate the way God created them, just as He created you.

I always thank God as I remember you in my prayers.
Philemon 4

Earthquake Tsunami Volcano Moments

Life is full of good and bad and we need to accept them both.

But what happens when the bad is less just "bad" and more akin to an "earthquake tsunami volcanic eruption?" What happens when a big blow comes?

Let's just be clear: a big blow *will* come.

If you haven't had one yet in your life, thank God for His grace and mercy. If you have, you know what I'm talking about. Because we all expect bad things to happen. We know people will get sick or the tire will be flat or the job might be lost.

But we don't expect *bad* things to happen.

See the importance of italics?

A bad thing we can handle. A *bad* thing—well, that messes you up big time. It rocks your world, causes major disruption of your health, home, and heart.

We don't *expect* earthquake tsunami volcanic eruptions, because if we lived expecting the really bad stuff to happen to us, we'd never get out of bed in the morning.

(At least I wouldn't. I'm not that brave.)

But what happens when the unexpected happens?

What happens when you when you find out your job is being outsourced? When your spouse tells you he is in love with someone else? When your doctor says the surgery wasn't successful? When the bank account is nearly empty and you still need to pay the mortgage? When you feel the upheaval of your world in a manner of seconds, what do you do?

I'm not going to say it will be easy.

I've faced enough of these moments over the last few years of my life that I'm going to do you a favor and treat you with honesty and respect. I will avoid the trite and super-Christian answer you've probably heard a few times in your life already: "God will take care of you."

I want to be clear that I truly do believe that. I truly do believe that if we ask Him to, God will take care of us. I've seen Him do it often enough in my own life that I know it's true—He *will* take care of you. But I also want to acknowledge that it's probably not what you want to hear when your life is in upheaval and you're facing an earthquake tsunami volcanic eruption moment.

Sometimes the right words at the wrong moment hurt more than they help.

"Hey, I know that the earthquake leveled your house, the volcano buried what matters the most to you, and you're trying to escape a tsunami. Just wanted to let you know, God will take care of you."

I'd almost deserve the punch in the face.

I'm also not going to say, "Let it go. Accept it and move on."

I won't say that because it's something I've never done.

I didn't do it when my grandfather died after complications from heart surgery. I didn't do it when my mother-in-law passed away after a decade-long battle with non-Hodgkin's lymphoma.

I didn't do it when I lost my job or when I lost dear friendships.

No, I did not just accept it.

I raged and got angry and sad and quiet and loud and yelled and prayed and cried. When the big blows come, it's okay to not be "okay." It's okay to hurt and cry and moan. It's okay to feel all those emotions that rage inside you, because they are natural and normal. They are entirely human responses to the truly horrible times in life.

So naturally, here's where I'm going to say, "Let go."

But I don't mean it the way I have elsewhere in this book.

I honestly mean, let go. Wander in the emotions and thoughts and worries and feelings and mood swings. Feel the depths and love the highs. This is just another journey you're on right now, and you need to let the road take you where it will. So, let go.

Eventually, you *will* come to a place where you can accept the pain and sorrow and anger. You will get to a place where you can accept that the hurt has happened and that this wound will one day scar over, too.

Please be real with yourself.

Now, be real with your Heavenly Father, too.

He already knows—He is just waiting for you to finally say something and be willing to let go and have Him do what only He can.

He is big enough and strong enough to carry the deepest and heaviest burdens of your soul. He doesn't mind if you yell at Him (case in point, half the Psalms—David had a *lot* of angst and anger toward God—he rails constantly about the unfairness of life, how horrible his enemies are, and the things he wishes for the people that hurt him are downright awful).

God is okay with our raging, and okay with our doubt.

Just remember, when it's all over and you have yelled and cried and shouted at God, He may answer you the way He answered Job:

"Who is this that obscures my plans with words without knowledge? Brace yourself like a man; I will question you, and you shall answer me." (Job 38:2-3)

God will let you rail and rant.

But He may also remind you that the words we freely let fly in the storm come from our lack of understanding or knowledge. We don't know His ways, we can't fathom His plans. He may tell you to buckle up, because it's just going to get harder. (Yes, this will not be an answer you want. I know because I've been getting that answer more often than I would like.)

But there's also good news.

He also says that He will turn your sadness into joy.

"You have turned my mourning into joyful dancing. You have taken away my clothes of mourning and clothed me with joy." (Psalm 30:11, NLT)

He will give you hope and courage and help you rest.

"Having hope will give you courage. You will be protected and will rest in safety." (Job 11:18, NLT)

He will wipe away every tear from your eyes.

"He will wipe every tear from their eyes, and there will be no more death or sorrow or crying or pain. All these things are gone forever." (Revelation 21:4, NLT)

Like any father, He may remind you after you've ranted and railed, that He is in charge, not you—but then He will pull you close and smother you in His embrace and remind you that He loves you more than you can possibly understand.

A big blow will come, my friend.

It may be an earthquake, it may be a tsunami, it may be both with an extra helping of volcanic eruption. Whatever it is, accept that God is more than okay with the feelings and emotions they bring out in you.

I will turn their mourning into gladness,
I will give them comfort and joy instead of sorrow.
(Jeremiah 31:13b)

I am Not a Hoarder

I have a confession to make.

(I think you probably just chuckled. I get it, I've already made a lot of confessions here. But at least I'm honest, right?)

I have a hard time getting rid of things.

I'm not a hoarder, but I do like to hang on to things from the past.

Not the figurative ones, but actual things.

Like ticket stubs from movies, room keys from hotels, guide maps from National Parks. I like those things because they remind me of great moments and memories I've shared with people I love.

On my desk as I write these words, I have a button from a Disneyland visit, a card from my daughter's college, a ring that belonged to my grandfather, a tumbler from "Hell's Kitchen" in Las Vegas from a recent trip with Robyn.

I should probably get rid of them, but they remind me of wonderful things.

And when I'm working on less than wonderful things, I like seeing them.

Those types of things you can probably understand. They have sentimental value. But what about the stuff that I should have gotten rid of a while ago? Those things Robyn frequently points out and says, "Why do you still have this?"

Things like clothes I've had too long, books I didn't really like, and so much other "stuff" that when I run out of room at my desk or on my bookshelf or closet, I take it out to the garage.

Our garage at times turns into a dangerous place.

Honestly, it can be like a trap-filled temple from an Indiana Jones movie. Like the opening scene from *Raiders of the Lost Ark*, I balance each piece carefully, because there is a giant boulder of death just waiting to fall from above. (Only the giant boulder of death is actually a precariously balanced stack of suitcases, and it's waiting to fall on me when I get out of the van.)

I know I'm not alone, because all of us have stuff we have a hard time letting go of. Your thing may not be books or ticket stubs. Your thing may be tools, even if they are slightly broken and the blades are warped. Your thing may be spices, even if the bottles are half empty and you haven't used that Australian wattleseed in 10 years.

You may be one of those people who save magazines because your kids might need them for a project someday, except your kids moved out several years ago and people just download everything from the internet anyway.

Stuff is easy to collect—it's harder to let go of.

Case in point? My compact disc collection, started in 1987. The first two cd's I purchased were *The Untouchables* soundtrack and *The Collection* by Amy Grant.

Since then, it's grown to over a thousand stacks in my closet. Which I haven't touched because I play everything digitally now. Why do I still have them stacked in my closet? Why haven't I just donated them and moved on? Because I really don't like to let go.

The sentimental stuff on my desk? It's in the way. I can't move my mouse very well, I can't see the notes from my last conference call, and now I have two tumblers on my desk because I forgot about the one with Gordon Ramsay staring at me. The stuff may have value in some way, but it sure has cluttered up my life.

This is what stuff does.

It gets in the way of our lives, cluttering up our homes and eventually our hearts and heads. Can't find things you actually need because you kept too much stuff that you didn't? Afraid to open the attic and put away what needs to be put away because you know it's become overrun with things you just wanted to put away and never looked at again?

That drawer in your kitchen?

The "junk" drawer?

Why do you have a drawer full of stuff you literally call "junk?" The very contents of the drawer are telling you, "Get rid of me! You don't need me!"

There's so much stuff in our lives that it's become our thing.

Managing the stuff.

We buy organization systems, rent storage facilities, and find nooks and crannies to stuff the stuff into. The stuff, and taking care of it, is a full-time gig, consuming our time and energy. It's our thing.

God never wants our stuff to become our thing.

He wants to be our thing.

In fact, Jesus says people who strive for that—people who make going after God their main purpose in life—are going to be blessed.

He doesn't use the term "go after God," because there's an actual word for that. It's called *righteousness*. Desiring to love, serve, praise, worship, be with, and experience God is what He wants for us.

"Blessed are those who hunger and thirst for righteousness, for they will be filled." (Matthew 5:6, NIV)

You will *never* get your fill of stuff.

But Jesus promises that we *will* be filled if make God our number one thing. Instead of trying to fill our lives with things that will not last, we need to hunger and thirst for what *really* matters.

When we have so much stuff competing for our attention or love or just plain distracting us because we keep tripping over it, we don't let Him have the space in our lives that He deserves. And honestly, the more we have, the more time it takes to manage it all. How does time with God fit in there? How do we have room in our hearts for Him when we barely have room in our garages to turn around?

God is saying, "I'll supply all you need. So forget the rest."

It's time to let that stuff go.

Acceptance says, "What I have is enough. I don't need more."

Adding stuff just because you can doesn't mean you should. Empty the closets of your home, clean out the garage. Take a trip or seven to your local charity and donate all the stuff you've stopped using. The books you'll never read again, clothes you haven't fit into for years, toys your kids outgrew a decade ago.

Bid them farewell.

And don't buy anything new until you get rid of something you stopped using awhile ago.

Simplify your life, get rid of the stuff, and you'll discover that there is peace in empty spaces. Like a much-needed break from work, giving your home some empty spaces clear the mind. It gives you room to breathe, to walk around (sometimes literally), and appreciate the things you have that you actually need and use. It can also free up your relationships with the people you live with. (Seriously. You should see my wife's face light up when I say the magic words, "I took a load of stuff to Goodwill today!")

Today, what can you get rid of to start simplifying your life?

I'm going to clean up my desk. Bye-bye, Gordon Ramsay. Grandpa's ring, you're going back into the box where you belong. Disneyland button, I have twelve of you already, so you need to go.

Oh, and the compact disc stacks? As hard as it may be for me to let them go, it's time. I haven't listened to an actual compact disc in years. So, they are going goodbye, too—after I make sure I've ripped their contents to my iTunes.

What will *you* do?

If you're not sure, ask God to give you a little insight—or ask a friend or family member. They know what the clutter is in your life, and they've been waiting for you to ask.

You will keep in perfect peace him whose mind is steadfast,
because he trusts in you.
(Isaiah 26:3)

Yard Work is Hard Work

You can tell when spring comes to the Pacific Northwest.

When the weather turns warmer, people in Seattle tend to head to the home improvement store. After the long days of grey, they desperately need something to brighten their lives. They look everywhere for their sunglasses, wipe the moss off their gardening clogs, and get out the gardening tools.

They wander the aisles of the garden center looking for the perfect flowers for their yards and get excited over different kinds of mulch. My wife is one of those people.

She loves yard work. And honestly, the only reason we have any beauty in our backyard is because she likes the work. She thrives on it. It fills her with joy and everything about "gardening" is something she loves.

This is not true for me.

Yard work rhymes with "hard work" and after several months of frost and snow and rain, the ground around our house is impossibly muddy, or hard as clay or whatever other words people who know things about dirt use to describe dirt that is impossible to work with.

I try to get excited about it and start to dig a hole for a new plant or pull up weeds that have overtaken flowerbeds, and I realize that it's not fun.

It's dirty and messy and hard and it takes *forever.*

I mean that literally.

Why does yard work seem to take four hundred hours on a nice Saturday?

The minute I start working in the yard, time itself slows down. I sit down to play a video game for twenty minutes and I look at the clock and two hours have gone by. Dinner out with friends seems to fly by. Even a relaxing afternoon on the deck in the summer zooms along.

But yard work? It's like entering *The Matrix* and watching everything around you move at a snail's pace.

And because I don't really enjoy it anyway, and it feels like it takes forever, I get frustrated. I get irritated. While I am sweating and fuming and maybe letting fly with an acceptable expletive (you know, "Holy crap!" or "Frickin' dirt, I hate you so much!"), Robyn is happily digging, slogging through it with her garden clogs and gloves and cute little shears.

I'm the poster child for anger.

She is the picture of happiness.

Which one of us is excelling at acceptance at this moment?

Life's struggles and difficult moments tend to be like that.

If you view your life (or your yard) as giant series of problems to overcome, you'll think you need to battle with it.

Like you, I also don't enjoy the harder moments in my life.

I pretend that I'm okay with everything and that it doesn't bother me. But then I get lost in the worries and the fears. I know I need to get rid of them, so I battle against them. And just like weeds, the tough moments in life fight back. They enjoy the stronghold they have, and they don't give up easily.

So we fight with them, rage at them, battle them. And then we get overwhelmed by them and say, "Forget it. It's not worth the fight." Then the weeds win, the flowerbed looks awful, and you get a letter from your Homeowner's Association.

Like a flowerbed with a weed problem, when our lives fill up with trouble, we need to accept the situation and deal with it. Put on the gloves, set aside time, and don't rush.

Pulling on weeds too hard will leave roots you'll just have to deal with again later. In the same way, fighting with the problem won't get rid of it. Sure, you may get out some surface anger or trouble, but the root? The root is still in there, deep, and it will just grow back.

Honestly, the only way to truly deal with the problem is to handle it the same way you would handle a weed: taking your time, handling it correctly, and making sure you get the root out. (And if all else fails, spray it with poison and kill it with fire.)

God created us to live in moments like this.

Even better, He gives us wisdom and clarity to understand what we should do and what our response should be. Our messy lives aren't surprises to Him, because He's seen everything.

Honestly. There's nothing we can do or cause to happen in our lives that surprises Him.

He's seen it all.

He's seen the beautiful yards, the overgrown ones, and everything in between. Your life's messy yard is where He does His best work, and where He excels. He created the grass and the flowers, the vegetables and the trees. He knows each plant by name and how to care for it. And like a master gardener, He knows exactly what tools we need to prune the problem, root out the mess, and return our lives to the glorious, colorful, beautiful state He created them to be.

If you like this metaphor, good. I didn't come up with it.

Jesus calls His Father the gardener in the Gospel of John.

"My Father is the gardener. He cuts off every branch of mine that doesn't produce fruit, and he prunes the branches that do bear fruit so they will produce even more." (John 15:1-2, NLT)

God knows what the garden needs.

He knows what to cut, what not to cut. He knows how to care for the plant to produce a harvest.

So why do I think I know better than Him?

When I hack and rush and try to get the problem taken care of quickly, I make it more difficult and leave a greater mess. I frustrate myself and I frustrate the gardener in charge because I am not following the plan or using the proper tools.

At home, I need to trust my wife when we start doing yard work together. She has a plan, she gave me the right tool for the job, and she will help me get to the best result possible if I just listen to her. When I do, our yard looks amazing. It's almost as if she really knows what she is doing.

(She does.)

In my trouble or problem, I need to trust that God also knows what He is doing. He will not let the trouble overcome me, the messiness get in the way of His goals. He won't let me mess everything up by ranting and raging, and He *will* remind me that He is in charge. Sometimes He'll do it nicely, by directing my focus to Him. Sometimes He'll do it the hard way, and smack me on the head with a garden rake. (Metaphorically speaking, of course.)

When I accept where I am and address the problem with God's plan, I can find more joy in the moment. When I let go of my frustration with the situation, when I stop holding on to what I think is best and accept that He has a better idea for what should happen, I can find more happiness in the situation.

Same thing goes for yard work.

But I'm not going to get clogs.

To Him who is able to keep you from falling and to present you before his glorious presence without fault and with great joy.
(Jude 24)

Just Make Believe You're a Tiny Little Seed

Many years ago, Robyn and I planted our first garden.

We were in the middle of a production set in the 1940's, so we called it our Victory Garden. We planted it in the side yard of the house were living in at the time. We had a great time.

If you remember what I said previously, you'll understand that when I say "we" I really mean "she" had a great time. She did most of the work planting a garden and I just came along for the free food. (I obviously wasn't raised on a farm, because I didn't realize that the free food comes along several months later and after a lot of hard work.)

My wife *really* loves gardening.

She loves getting her hands right into the dirt.

As soon as the weather changes, she's planning trips to the garden section of Home Depot and dreaming of geraniums and other flowers.

I love to say, "A man's got to have land, Shannon" in my best Tom Cruise Irish accent when she starts getting her hands right into the dirt.

(That's a quote from *Far and Away*, a movie about Irish potato farmers who get involved with boxing and the Oklahoma land race, and Tom Cruise uses an Irish accent in it. Of course, nothing makes you seem timelier than a reference to film that nobody has seen since the early 1990's. Back to the book.)

Planting a garden is a process.

We turn the soil, pull out rocks, kill the weeds, add new manure fertilizer (bringing the scent of the dairy farm to your suburban neighborhood) and make a plan for where everything should go. I actually only help with the first four.

I get to turn soil.

I pull out rocks and kill weeds.

I also get to lay the manure. (Which means I get to do my best Biff Tannen impression and say, "I hate manure." That's a reference to the bad guy from the *Back to the Future* movies. He really doesn't like manure.)

I do not get a say in the plan, and that's ok, because I have no idea how to make it all work together. I don't know why tomatoes should be next to carrots or why we plant that flower around the edge to keep the slugs away. I may be able to work well with computers and talk in front of crowds of people, but laying out a garden?

Makes no sense to me.

My wife understands it. Robyn looks at the bit of land we have filled with soil and prepared for seeds and knows where everything should go and how it all works together.

She knows exactly what it will take for every seed she plants to turn into a thriving, growing plant that produces enough vegetables for us to enjoy as a family every summer and fall.

You probably know where I'm going with this, because it's a great metaphor for life. For us to become all we were created to be, we are going to have to go through some tough times. There's an old song from the original "Listen to the Land" attraction at Epcot in Walt Disney World that says it best: "Just make believe you're a tiny little seed."

Go ahead, do it. I'll wait.

Now that you see yourself as a seed (way to use your imagination!), you recognize that a seed might love to stay cozy and warm in its packaging, but for it to actually become a tomato, it *has* to be planted. It's gotta get down in the dirt where it's messy and smelly. Oh, surprise, it's going to get broken, too!

The seed has to break open for the plant to actually grow.

Same thing goes for us. Most of us would *love* to stay cozy and warm and safe and never have any trouble at all. After all, who would choose to leave the comfort and warmth to get down in the dirt? Who would choose messy over nice and clean? Who chooses stinky over lovely?

Nobody.

And yet, that's what it's going to take for us to become who God has created us to be.

God doesn't put you in hard places to mess you up.

He doesn't take you out of your comfort zone because He enjoys watching you squirm. That's not what God does. He's not vindictive or cruel. Like a master gardener who knows what is best for the seed, God knows what exactly what you need. He knows the best way to help you transform and grow and become what He created you to be. And since He created and cares for you, He will do whatever it takes to help you fulfill your destiny.

The Bible doesn't use the word destiny. Instead, the concept is presented beautifully by Paul in Philippians.

"And I am certain that God, who began the good work within you, will continue his work until it is finally finished on the day when Christ Jesus returns." (Philippians 1:2, NLT)

We use the word destiny but it's really God starting something in you and making sure it is complete. But just to make sure you get the work being done, I want point out the adjective describing the work, because it's important.

The word there is "good."

He began a "good work" in you.

In the original Greek, the word is *agathos*. It means "intrinsically good, good in nature, good whether it be seen to be so or not." Which means that the work God is doing, even in the hard or difficult moments, is by its very nature good. It can't help but be good, and whether or not we see that it is good, *it is good.*

95

That's why God does what He does.

He does it because it's the only way to get you to become who you truly are meant to be.

You don't grow in only good times and happy moments.

You need the hard and difficult times, too. Seeds need sunshine—and rain. Seeds need warmth and light, but they also need darkness and clouds. Whether it's a great day in the garden or a difficult one, it is still *good*.

Back to our victory garden.

I may not have understood it, but in the end, Robyn's plan was great. It took work to get it going, and it took work to help it grow. We watered the garden and fed it—we pulled out weeds and had to keep the rabbits out. But in the end, we had tomatoes and cucumbers and pumpkins. We enjoyed lettuce from our own garden. Everything that happened to those tiny seeds turned out for their good (and ours).

Accept the difficult place.

It's your garden. It's the place where you will be able to grow.

Realizing that the difficult place may actually be for your benefit is a huge step toward letting go. Eventually, you will bloom and you'll discover that the pain had a purpose.

It was no accident.

It was meant to happen, and there is a reason for it.

Remember, for the gardener to get the best out of the garden, there has to be a plan and a purpose for every seed. For you to become all that God created you to be, you have to see His plan and purpose for you.

He's helping complete the good work he started in you.

So relax in that.

Just see yourself as that tiny little seed.

And remember, the stuff that grows out of the seed is usually much better, tastier, prettier, and just more awesome than it was when it was just a seed.

The same thing goes for you, too.

Endure hardship with us like a good soldier of Christ Jesus.
(2 Timothy 2:3)

The (Un) Joy of Running

The farther you get in the journey toward accepting who you are and where you are, the more you might discover it's like a long-distance race.

Finishing well isn't about how fast you run at the beginning, it's about pacing yourself and taking time to speed up and slow down as necessary.

(I know this because I've seen people run.)

When you go running with someone you care about, it's a little more fun. Especially if you're the one who doesn't really enjoy running. I've experienced this a few times with my wife. She loves running, and she loves running alone. I don't enjoy running, so running alone is torture. When she is gracious enough to let me come with her, I enjoy it a lot more.

I think she does *not* enjoy it when I come with her.

I think that because she actually said, "I don't enjoy it."

She is not subtle.

The point is this: when you're going through something painful and achy, like running when it's not your thing, it's a lot easier to do it with someone who is good at it. They know better the bends and curves in the road. They know how to pace themselves and will warn you when you're pushing too hard.

They don't mind if you fall behind a bit, because they look over their shoulder and encourage you. Even better, they realize it's not a race.

Nobody is going to "win" this, because it's just a run.

Life is like that.

All of us are on a run, and some of us are novices (like me) and some of us enjoy it because you are crazy (like my wife). When you're hurting on the run, giving up and quitting isn't really an option, because you've got to keep moving to get home. You can stop on the side of the road, sure. But if you want to get where you're going, you have to *keep* going.

There are a couple different ways to help make that happen.

(Do not follow the example of Michael Scott in *The Office*, who fueled for his *Michael Scott's Dunder Mifflin Scranton Meredith Palmer Celebrity Rabies Awareness Pro-Am Fun Run Race for the Cure* by eating a huge plate of fettucine alfredo. That is never the way to keep going on your race, and it really grosses people out when you get sick at the end. Kind of like life.)

Having someone alongside, or even slightly ahead, who shouts encouraging words and gives you pointers about how to do it well?

That's awesome!

Like that incredible opening scene from *Chariots of Fire*, you feel like an Olympic champion, an iconic score running through your head. You hold your head up, throw your shoulders back and you run like you've never run before.

The opposite version of that is also motivating, but for different reasons.

The person alongside or slightly ahead is still there, but they aren't shouting encouraging words. They're yelling at you to not be such a pansy, that you're not going to die, and you better get moving, maggot! I know this motivation works, too, because I've seen *Platoon* and other movies with drill sergeants.

The second one is more along the lines of my own experience.

I'm not a runner, and when I force myself on runs with my wife, this is how she motivates my usually-desk-bound body. Robyn really prefers to run alone. And by prefers, I mean in twenty years of marriage, I've gone running with her twice. If I'm going to move in on her thing, I have to accept her way of doing it.

However it happens, though, having that other person with you is a good thing.

It may not make the run any less painful, but it sure makes it more do-able and at least a lot more motivational to not quit and give up. (At least for those of us who don't enjoy running and need lots of positive reinforcement.) You may not love it, you may hate moments of it, but when you see that person ahead of you and they finally give you the universal sign of "you got this," you know you can make it.

That'd be a thumbs up, by the way.

God is giving you the thumbs up sign every day. And He will use both versions of motivation to help get you where you're going. Sometimes He's shouting encouraging words at you. He's all smiles and sunshine and reminding you that you're loved and cared for and "You can do it!"

Joshua 1:9 is a great verse to consider in those moments when you need to hear God's encouraging voice. *This is my command—be strong and courageous! Do not be afraid or discouraged. For the Lord your God is with you wherever you go." (Joshua 1:9, NLT)*

That's what God said to Joshua when he wasn't sure he could handle the job of leading the people of Israel into the Promised Land. God says that to you, too. The promise of God being with us, wherever we go, wasn't just for Joshua.

It's for all of us today, too.

Sometimes, though, God may need to encourage you by using a bit harsher words and experiences. Oh, God is never going to call you maggot or tell you to "Move your rear end, meatball!" But He will use harder moments and circumstances to keep you from stopping in the place you're not supposed to be.

If you want an example of this from the Bible, read the entire book of Exodus. It starts out amazing, and then it gets pretty ugly.

God does an amazing thing in the lives of His people and they complain so much He blows His top. Like the dad who yells into the backseat, "If I hear *one more word,* I am turning this car around!"

God says, *"That's it! I've had enough complaining!"*

But instead of turning the car around, He just lets the car wander around the desert for 40 years.

Whatever form of encouragement God uses, trust that He's still going to be there along the way. He may be a little farther ahead sometimes, but that's okay. He's farther ahead because He knows the road better than you. He created it, after all. So when you look up and He seems distant, it's only because He's waiting at the next point on the run.

He may judge your form.

He may yell at you about keeping up.

But His presence just reminds you that you're not alone.

I will be honest: after a great run, my wife comes home hot and sweaty. I still love her to death, but she looks angry and mean. She looks like she wants to punch the world in the face until it cries for mercy. And if one of the kids asks, "Did you have a nice run?" she will reply, "Nobody ever has a *nice* run."

The truth is, it will get tough at times.

It will be painful and achy.

You will want to quit.

Just lift your eyes up and see that God is there, right there ahead of you. Wherever the run takes you, no matter how many times you come and go, you've got a partner. He's giving you the thumbs up, so don't give up.

You got this.

He will not let your foot slip—he who watches over you will not slumber.
Psalm 121:3

When Your Maps App Doesn't Work

Have you ever gotten on a road you weren't sure about?

In these days of GPS and our phones giving us turn by turn directions, it's a little harder to get lost. But what if you end up in a place where there is no network service (a horrifying place, indeed) and you have to pull out an old-fashioned map and figure out where you were going?

That happened to us a few years ago.

One of our favorite things to do is take road trips. (I may have mentioned this a few times already.) And when we aren't driving to Disneyland, we're exploring America's "Best Idea," the National Parks.

We love these places and have driven to nearly 100 of them over the past 14 years. Our love for the National Parks really began in 2006, with a road trip over 3,000 miles long across the American West.

Since then, we've visited the big and well-known National Parks, like Grand Canyon National Park, Glacier National Park, Yellowstone and Yosemite.

We've visited a few of the lesser-known ones, too. Craters of the Moon, Pipe Spring, Mesa Verde. All of them are unique and beautiful, full of natural beauty or amazing history. And all of them are usually way out in the middle of nowhere, far from the closest cell phone tower.

But a few years ago, it was really bad.

We had just visited a National Monument in the remote southwest corner of Idaho. It's literally at the end of the highway, and the only way out of it is to drive the unpaved roads into Utah or turn around and go back. City of Rocks National Monument is a pretty cool place until you are trying to get back to the small highway you came in on and your cell phone has the dreaded "No Service" notification. Then panic sets in when you realize that you don't have a map, except for the souvenir one your son picked up from Cracker Barrel—which says, right on it, "Not to scale. Do not use for navigation."

Let's just say relationships were tested.

Words were spoken.

With intensity.

Robyn and I both handled the situation differently, and neither of us came out perfectly. Our kids looked at us trying to read a cartoon map and heard us speaking with less-than-loving tones and knew something bad was happening.

Luckily, we kept driving the way we'd come in and eventually, we had a cellular signal. And when the signal showed up, so did the highway.

Argument over, it was time to hit the highway again.

When we lose our directions on the road it's one thing—we can usually drive long enough and far enough until we find someone or someplace that will help you until Siri shows up again.

When it happens in life, it's a whole different story.

Once our lives hit a pretty clear trajectory, we set it in cruise control and just accept that we will hit the destination after a steady speed of 65 mph and a few hours. But when the road closes and we are forced off into a side street we've never been on?

Panic ensues.

Most of us struggle with accepting change or bends in the road or unexpected moments because it's not *in the plan*. We find ourselves in an unfamiliar neighborhood without a map or a guide and moan, "This is *not* what was supposed to happen."

And God looks at us and says, "Excuse me? Whose plan is this, anyway?"

We pull out our GPS and point out the destination. He gently takes it out of our hands and instead pulls out a giant, ancient roadmap. It's got markings everywhere—the best routes, the best restaurants, the rest stops where you won't get an infection, the best sights to see along the way—because He has travelled every inch of the road and knows exactly the best route for *you*.

Your plan doesn't include rest stops and random crazy hotels or the all-you-can-pancake buffet. But God's plan does. His plan includes all that because He *knows* you'll need the rest stop. He *knows* the weird hotel night will make a great family story. And I am just guessing, but I'm sure He *loves* pancakes.

If your GPS isn't working right now and you feel like you're a bit lost, ask God where He is taking you. He knows. He mapped it all out ahead of time, and He is honestly waiting, excited, for you to say, "Hey God, can you please show me the way to go?"

The prayers in the Bible where people do this?

Usually turns out pretty incredible for them—even if it's not what they originally thought was going to happen.

Ask Joshua. He prayed for help leading the children of Israel and God used him to conquer giants and bring down the walls of Jericho.

Or Gideon. He prayed God would send a deliverer for His people, and God chose Him. And in spite of all the ways he tried to get out of it, God use Gideon and 300 men to defeat thousands.

Ask Esther. She prayed for courage to approach her husband, the most powerful ruler on earth, and saved her people from certain extermination.

Need another example? One of my favorites is Peter.

The man was a fisherman, busy doing his thing on a clear path and journey until Jesus showed up. He messed with Peter's plan so hard one day that it causes Peter to say something to God that not many of us would have the courage to say.

After Jesus miraculously helps him—and his brother Andrew and partners James and John—catch so many fish that it overloads the nest and nearly sinks their boat, Peter gets back to shore and knows something isn't right.

Peter just flat out says, *"Oh, Lord, please leave me—I'm such a sinful man." (Luke 5:8, NLT)*

Luckily for Peter—and for us—that's not how God works.

His plans and ideas are nothing like what we expect.

God makes that clear in the book of Isaiah.

"My thoughts are nothing like your thoughts," says the Lord. "And my ways are far beyond anything you could imagine." (Isaiah 55:8, NLT)

We expect God's plan and ideas to be at least somewhat akin to ours. We hope He's thinking what we're thinking. But He's not. He can't think like we do, focused on the here and now. We are worried about our lunch plans and God is looking at the entirety of eternity and seeing our place in His timeline.

God's plan will not be like ours.

And that is *okay*.

I never planned on doing any of the things I have done in my life. My plan in high school was to go to law school and become a lawyer. (I've never been to law school and I'm not a lawyer.)

Each of the girls I was *certain* were "the one" weren't even close, and the woman I eventually did marry was nothing like the type I thought I was going to be with the rest of my life. (And for that I could not be more thankful.)

The road I thought I was taking?

Turns out it wasn't even on the map.

I'm not saying your plan isn't good.

But I am saying His plan will always be better, because He knows you even better than you know yourself. The way He thinks and dream for you? Beyond what you can even imagine.

So turn off your GPS.

Trust the map maker, because He has a great trip planned for you.

"For I know the plans I have for you," declares the Lord,
"plans to prosper you and not to harm you,
plans to give you a hope and a future."
(Jeremiah 29:11)

Get That Kid a Band-Aid®

Have you ever been on a playground full of kids?

I used to watch my kids play during recess because there is something wonderful about watching a bunch of children running around and getting sweaty while they make up games and throw red balls at each other.

I loved recess when I was a kid, too.

I played football sometimes (not very well), foursquare a lot (I was the reigning champion of Seattle Christian School in 4th grade), and made up stories that a couple of friends and I would act out. Yes, that last one does seem a bit weird, but I did grow up to tell stories for a living, so it make sense.

The thing about recess is that kids get hurt a lot at recess.

If I was a teacher dismissing kids for recess, I would totally say, "May the odds ever be in your favor."

With all the running around and the balls flying everywhere and the gleeful abandon of not having to be sitting in a classroom, it kind of turns into *The Hunger Games* Junior out there.

There's lots of yelling and things being thrown. Kids are chasing each other across one area of the playground while others are jumping ropes. Packs of wild children run from one area to another. There are playground supervisors, but they mostly just watch as the kids' most primal instincts come out.

This is what happens on a playground.

It's kill or be killed.

Survival of the fittest.

Until someone gets hurt.

When a kid gets hurt, something kind of crazy and cool happens. (To be clear, it's not cool when a kid gets hurt. What happens after, though, is pretty amazing.)

All the activity around the kid stops.

The air grows still, the noise stops, and it's like they all sense one of their own has fallen. One by one, they begin to gather. When one kid gets hurt, the rest of the kids rush in and start helping.

They dig through their pockets for bandages and try to create splints out of twigs. They throw their arms around the other kid and help them get to the playground supervisor. And they don't go back to playing until they know the other kid is going to be okay—and also because they want to see a little bit of blood. (Kids are creepy that way.)

When adults see someone who is hurting, we are not like kids.

Instead of rushing into help, we form a circle around the wounded person and start asking questions. "Why did this happen?" or "What societal problem caused this?"

Before we can help, we have to make sure they are *for* the same things we are for. We have to ensure they are *against* the same things as us. And then, if they hit all the right criteria, we *may* offer them assistance.

Jesus actually ran into this personally while He was in Jerusalem. He and His disciples encountered a man who had been blind since birth. Instead of having compassion on the man, they treat him like a theological exercise.

"Why was this guy born this way?" they ask.

"Was it because of his own sins or his parents' sins?" (John 9:2, NLT)

Uhm, what?

If this had been a text conversation, Jesus' first response may have been the facepalm emoji. "You've got to be kidding me." The disciples have just acknowledged the man was *born* blind, and they still wonder if maybe *his own sins* were the cause. Jesus has a lot more grace than I do, and instead of calling them idiots, He answers:

"This happened so the power of God could be seen in him." (John 9:3, NLT)

The man was hurting. He'd been begging all his life. But instead of seeing him as the hurting and wounded person he was, they surrounded him and asked questions and eventually blamed him. Meanwhile, God looks at the wounded and says, "I'm going to show you some amazing things as you experience healing."

We are so much like the disciples.

We see someone hurt and try to understand and contemplate and come up with answers that fit our feelings about their hurts and wounds.

Kids see someone who is hurting and forget about social issues and concerns and how this works into the big picture of life. They see the bloody knee, the tears in the eyes. They look at another kid on the playground who is bloodied and bruised and know they have to do something.

So they shout, *"Get that guy a Band-Aid®!"*

Accepting that we are going to be wounded at times means we know it will happen to others, too. If we ignore them or try to make sure we help for the right reasons, we miss out on the opportunity to show them something they need to see, too: *acceptance.* How can they let go of their wound or hurt if the ones around them won't even give them a shoulder to lean on?

God doesn't analyze your political beliefs or your stand on an issue before He offers you hope and peace. He doesn't tell you to clean up your crap before He will let you lean on His shoulder. If He did, none of us would get help. None of us would have hope.

Instead, God sees the hurt or wound and points out why it's there: "So the glory of God can be seen." God is glorified when healing happens. When we are His hands and feet to the wounded and hurting around us, we show God's love and compassion—His glory—to the world.

Later in the story, everyone questions the man who was born blind.

Jesus healed him and gave him back his sight. But everyone freaks out about it. The religious leaders, his parents. They ask all sorts of questions, trying to figure out what happened.

The man's response is perfect.

"I was blind, and now I can see!" (John 9:25, NLT)

This should be our response, too.

He was listening to everything they said about what had happened to him. He hadn't seen anything, only heard and followed Jesus' commands. And when he did that, his life was changed forever.

He was saying to the leaders and others who were questioning him, "I don't know all the whys and wherefores. I don't know exactly how it happened or what occurred. I just know that I'm not the same person I was before."

We don't need to know the hows or whys.

We aren't given answers to the questions of how the wound happened or how likely it is to happen again. What we are given is an opportunity to make the difference only we can make in the life of someone else.

When God helps us in our wounded state, He's reminding us that there are plenty of hurting people around us who need us to help them, too.

We don't need to ask questions.

We don't need to understand the reason behind the hurt.

We are simply called to be the kids on the playground, running to help our fallen friend and not leaving until the wound is bandaged up.

When we see someone hurting next time, instead of asking them how it happened, simply shout,

"Hey! Get that guy a Band-Aid®!"

If one falls down, his friend can help him up.
(Ecclesiastes 4:10a)

The "Ers" of Life

The *ers*.

Nasty, nasty things to experience.

I'll admit, I've succumbed to a bad case of the *ers* before.

You probably have, too.

It's pretty common among a very unique subset of species, one you've probably heard of before.

Homo sapiens.

Yep, people everywhere suffer from the *ers*. If you've ever wished you were skinnier or taller, happier or richer, prettier or handsomer, wittier or funnier--or any of the other *ers* we throw out at times because we look in the mirror or at those around us and think, "If only I was...," then you've also been through the *ers*.

We typically do this because when we look in the mirror or think a lot about ourselves, we aren't big fans of what we see.

We may not particularly like the way our noses align on our face, or where we carry extra weight.

We aren't fans of how much money is currently in our checking account. We have lost the passion we once had for our jobs. That's when the *ers* show up, and the "If only's…" begin.

"If only I was richer."

"If only I was better loved."

"If only I was happier."

"If only I was…_____ er." (That's for your thing.)

The *ers* are awful things that cause us to look down on ourselves. And once we start looking down at ourselves, we are certain the people around are doing it, too. The clerk at the store? She's thinking, "If only this person smelled better." The grocery store cashier, "If only this person made healthier choices." You can almost *hear* them thinking it, right?

Guess what?

They aren't thinking it.

Most of the people around you don't think about you at all. And the people who *do* think about you actually think you're pretty awesome.

Struggling with thinking you're not the best parent?

Chances are your kids brag about you to their friends.

Wishing you had a better job?

I'll bet at least one person in your circle of relationships thinks what you do for a living is pretty cool and wishes they had a job as awesome as yours.

Thinking you could stand to lose some weight?

Okay, sure, maybe—but the people around you probably think you look pretty good. You get what I'm saying? You don't need to be perfect in any way, but you need to stop thinking about all the *ers* and start realizing that who you are right now is pretty darn good.

Acceptance of yourself means you looking at your life and finding all the things that are right. It's looking at yourself the way others do. And more importantly, the way God looks at you.

He doesn't view you as a loser.

In His eyes, you don't need to be any more *er* than you already are.

He made you, so He knows your faults and your foibles.

He knows where your strengths lie and where you struggle.

And He *still* says, "I like you. I care about you."

Need proof? Look at the entirety of the Bible. All of it is God's love story for you and me. From the beginning to the end, it's all about how much He loves us—and even when we screwed up the relationship, He stopped at nothing to make it right again. He kept pursuing us, even though we had given up.

In fact, His pursuit became His passion and drove Him to do the unexpected. He became one of us.

The King James Version of the Bible expresses that incredible love in the most beautiful language.

"For God so loved the world, that he gave his only begotten Son, that whosoever believeth in him should not perish, but have everlasting life." (John 3:16, KJV)

God thinks you're so awesome, He put Himself smack dab in the middle of our messy world. And even when He saw the mess, He stayed.

Because of His great love for you.

The *ers* will still come.

You can't escape them, because you are human.

It's part of the reality of who we are that we can't help ourselves sometimes. But when you start to feel the *er* coming on, tell it to be quiet. Don't entertain it with an "If only, either."

The only time "if only" ever mattered was taken care of. "If only someone loved me, then I'd be happier—joyfuller—smilier—peacefuller." (I made those last two up.) Someone *did* love you that much.

And He demonstrated it by coming to be with you. The only *ers* you need are the ones He gives you. The ones you get because God so loved this world—because God so loved *you.*

He showed it by giving up everything for you.

Romans 8:32: *"Since he did not spare even his own Son but gave him up for us all, won't he also give us everything else?" (NLT)*

Philippians 2:7: *"Instead, he gave up his divine privileges; he took the humble position of a slave and was born as a human being." (NLT)*

1 John 3:16: *"We know what real love is because Jesus gave up his life for us." (NLT)*

You don't need to be whatev*er* it is you think you need to be. You don't need whatev*er* it is you think you need.

God knows exactly what you need to be, where you need to be, and how to get you there. It's what He does for us every day.

So, stop the *er*-ing.

You don't need to be any more *er* than you already are—unless you're wondering if you could be any more awesom*er*. Because the people around you, and the One who made you, would say, "Nope. You're pretty darn awesome just the way you are."

> *Therefore, since we are surrounded by such a great cloud of witnesses,*
> *let us throw off everything that hinders and the sin that so easily entangles.*
> *And let us run with perseverance the race marked out for us.*
> *(Hebrews 12:1)*

The Joy of Not "Comparison Helping"

When you're in the middle of tough time or struggling with feelings of acceptance, it's very easy to turn all your focus inward. You've got *a lot* going on in your head, and most of it isn't great.

You've got negative thoughts running back and forth like a hyperactive kid after too much candy and video games. Worse, your head is racing while you don't feel like doing much. You'll find ways to stay busy, but puttering around the house or flipping through your phone for something to occupy your time won't help. When you're done playing that highly addictive mobile game, you're back to your head full of thoughts.

Honestly, I get it. It's tough to let go.

I started writing this book a year ago.

I've been struggling with the very things I'm writing about for 12 months—and probably more.

In the last year, I've been quieter, more thought-filled, and more introspective. And while I wish I could say it was healthy thinking, it's not.

I spent way too much of the last year in my head.

When you're struggling with accepting who and where you are, it can be tough to get *out* of your head. And if you've got that kind of temperament that people kindly "artistic," it's even harder because artists are some of the moodiest, most introspective people around. I don't know how anyone lives with them. (Ahem. I may or may not be speaking from personal experience here.)

Seriously, they can be huge jerks sometimes.

(Okay, it's me. I'm one of those people. And I *know* I'm hard to live with. Sorry, family.)

Want an easy way to get out of your head for awhile?

We've looked at a couple already.

Adjust your focus, right?

Don't be too mean to that reflection in the mirror.

If you really want to get out of your head and start letting go, here's another suggestion. Stop looking at yourself and start looking at other people.

Hang on, I don't mean that way.

Don't compare how awful their life is to yours, just so you'll feel better. That's not going to help you in any way.

(See earlier comment about jerks.)

Adjusting your focus so you spend time helping someone else is a great way to live a life of acceptance. You have skills and talents that God gave you—why not use them to better the life of another person?

You have time to kill right now?

Instead of hopping on your phone, hop in the car and offer your services somewhere.

All of us were created to help other people.

We *weren't* created to be selfish and sit around and mope and feel badly about our current situation. If you can't change your situation today, change your focus and start seeing the difference you can make in the life of someone else.

Remember, though.

This isn't "comparison helping."

"Comparison helping" is when you help someone worse off than you so you can compare your life to how horrible theirs is and feel better about yourself.

That's not what this is about.

This isn't about going to the homeless shelter and offering some clothes you don't want anymore because "they" could sure use the assistance. This is not taking the kids to help at the rescue mission's soup night because you're trying to show them how nice it feels to pour soup into a bowl being held by a sad old alcoholic. If you're helping just to compare and see how much better you are doing in life than somebody else, you're doing it wrong.

Help *anyone you can*, not just someone who might be "worse off" than you.

This isn't about making yourself feel superior to their place or position—this is about unselfishly using what God gave you right now to make a difference for someone else.

The Gospels show how Jesus models this for us.

Whether the person was important or not, rich or a beggar, slave or free, Jesus stopped and interacted with and made a difference in their lives. Each of them needed someone to care about their need, their fear, their worry—and He did it without worrying about what others would think or what it would do for Him.

The man born blind.

The woman who hadn't stopped bleeding for years.

The lepers on the outskirts of town.

The centurion, Jairus' daughter, Mary Magdalene.

Jesus stopped and helped and cared about all of these people.

Follow His example and get out of your head.

Stop thinking about yourself and how the world is affecting you and go out and affect your world. Make the difference that only you can make, that God has created you specifically and wonderfully to do.

What you have *right now*, even if it's not your ideal, can make the difference in someone else's life. Maybe you don't have the work you want to have right now because you need to use your time to bless someone else. Maybe you don't have the income you want to have right now because you need to give a little more freely.

Where you are right now?

It's where God has you.

On purpose.

I'm writing this to myself, too. I'm reminding myself to get out of my thoughts and fears and worries and get busy helping others.

Helping people I love who need help—caring for hurting people around me—taking time to check in and make sure people are okay. This is what I can do *right now*.

If you think you've got too much going on to help someone else right now, let's look back to Jesus. In the middle of His worst day, He still stopped and helped someone who was hurting.

Jesus has wrestled all night with what is to come. He's in the garden with His best friends, all of whom are so clueless to His pain and thoughts that they've fallen asleep. When Judas and the temple guards show up to arrest Him, all hell breaks loose.

Peter, the fisherman, starts brandishing a sword.

A sword.

(There's never enough attention paid to this. Where did he get it? Why does he suddenly have one when there's never been a reference to it before? And is it any wonder what happens next?) Swinging it wildly, Peter cuts a guy's ear off.

Jesus is about to bound and carted off to trial, but He stops everything and goes to the wounded man. I am sure Jesus looked him in the eye. He saw his pain, saw the blood, and heard his cry for help and scream of agony.

Jesus sees the wounded man. But He doesn't say, "Hey, man. Hope that heals. I'd like to help, but I'm in a really bad place right now. Maybe in three days?"

There, as the worst 24 hours of His life is about to kick into high gear, He heals the man's ear. He does what only He could do right then, in that moment.

What an incredible moment. What an incredible example!

When you're not sure about yourself and what's going on and think you're too overwhelmed by your own stuff to help someone, do what He did.

Stop and help someone else, not because of what it will do for you—but because of what it can mean for them.

Give, and it will be given to you.
A good measure, pressed down, shaken together and running over, will be poured
into your lap. For with the measure you use, it will be measured to you.
(Luke 6:38)

Find Your Summertime Patio

My wife and I love sitting outside in warm weather.

Because we live in Seattle, that means we get about 10 days a year to do it. (Okay, that was hyperbole. We can get about 60 truly amazing days a year where there is no better place on earth to live. The other 305? Not so much.)

When we first moved into our house, we doubled the size of our postage stamp-sized patio with paving bricks and slowly turned it into what we called "Summertime Patio."

It had string lights, comfortable seating, outdoor music, and a nice gurgling fountain. We'd sit out on it in nice weather and pretend we were sitting at Trader Sam's at The Disneyland Hotel. (If you've never been, I highly recommend it.)

A couple years ago, we decided to expand it.

Working with one of my best friends, we designed and built our own deck which actually was twice the size of our living room. We love being out there so much that it's the biggest "room" in our house.

We still call it "Summertime Patio" because "Summertime Deck" just doesn't have the same ring to it. On any even slightly warm day where we can, our entire family sits out there. We tell stories, laugh, eat dinner, have a drink or two, and make memories.

When friends come over in the summer, we all sit outside.

What is your "Summertime Patio?"

What place in your life do you retreat to when you need to just relax and unwind and disconnect? This is important because when you begin to accept where you are and who you are today, you'll realize that you've missed out on something because you didn't let go.

You missed out on relaxation.

You can't calm down when you're desperately hanging on. Someone who has let go and is no longer clinging finds their muscles suddenly at rest. They realize their breathing comes easier.

When that comes, where you will sit and reflect?

And honestly, don't pick a place where a screen is the number one feature. I get you might want your phone nearby, but avoid places where screens are prominent. Whenever a screen is in a room, everyone wants it to be *on*. And if a screen is on, you're watching it.

I know this because in those moments when we go to restaurants with screens on, and even if the only thing on is some random show on ESPN, a channel I would never watch at home and only subscribe to because it's required, I *can't look away*.

So, no screens.

Because the point of your personal Summertime Patio is to be *off*. Your brain has been racing, your heart has been anxious, and you're finally accepting things and letting go—and that means disconnecting. The thing is, when you accept who you are, it's time to do what you've put off doing for so long.

Relax.

Find your Summertime Patio and kick back.

If you like a drink now and then, have one. Sit there with people you really enjoy being around. Laugh over stupid jokes. Eat a meal. Stay out at long as you can. (There's nothing better than watching the sun slowly set from Summertime Patio as the music from a majestic film score plays in the background.)

You were created for rest.

You were created for relaxation.

And the stress and worry and fear that you've been carrying wasn't meant for you to carry in the first place. When we rest, we lay those things aside—at least for a little while—and are rewarded with calmer hearts and heads.

God encourages us to rest.

"My people will live in safety, quietly at home. They will be at rest." (Isaiah 32:18, NLT)

"Then Jesus said, 'Come to me, all of you who are weary and carry heavy burdens, and I will give you rest.'" (Matthew 11:28, NLT)

"Then Jesus said, 'Let's go off by ourselves to a quiet place and rest awhile.'" (Mark 6:31, NLT)

"No wonder my heart is glad, and my tongue shouts his praises! My body rests in hope." (Acts 2:26, NLT)

Get it? Rest and relaxation are godly pursuits.

And if you still struggle with these examples, I have a better one.

Jesus Himself sets the example for rest.

Jesus had his Summertime Patio when He relaxed and hung out at the home of His friends Lazarus, Mary, and Martha. There's a moment in His story that shows this, even though we don't realize it.

In Luke 10, as Jesus and His friends are on their way to Jerusalem, they stop for the night at their friends' house in Bethany. Martha complains about the lack of help from her sister, and Jesus gently scolds her. But right there in the scripture it says, *"Martha was distracted by the big dinner she was preparing." (Luke 10:40a)* It's not just another opportunity to teach, it's a dinner party!

Jesus got away from the noise and crowd often during His ministry. After He fed 5,000 men with a boy's sack lunch, He sent everyone away and went off by Himself. He was there so long that night fell as the disciples cross the lake.

"After sending them home, He went up into the hills by Himself to pray. Night fell while He was there alone." (Matthew 14:23, NLT)

Jesus took naps!

This makes my wife happy, because she loves naps. So, clearly, Robyn is more like Jesus than I am, because I have never liked naps. There are better ways to rest, I think—but usually, while she is resting during a nap, I'm busy doing something. So napping is godly, and clearly a good thing.

Before He calms the storm, the Bible makes clear Jesus is snoozing. *"As they sailed across, Jesus settled down for a nap." (Luke 8:23, NLT)* Settling down for a nap is a commitment to rest and sleep and getting away from it all. Sure, the disciples were about to start freaking out over the storm, but Jesus was able to lie there, *sound asleep* in the boat as it tossed and turned. If you are someone who loves naps, this is your favorite Bible story.

And honestly, if you think you're too busy for a little down time, you're kind of saying you're busier than Jesus. Which you know is not true.

Acceptance frees you to enjoy life, to stop and just sit for awhile. So, let go, unwind, and *rest.*

And give that place a cool name.

But you can't use Summertime Patio, because that's ours.

He seldom reflects on the days of his life,
because God keeps him occupied with gladness of heart.
Ecclesiastes 5:20

Letting Go So Your Family Gets Your Best You

Author's Note: This one is pretty important. At least I discovered it was for me. On my journey to letting go, this one really made a huge difference, and I hope it makes a difference for you, too.

When you start to let go, it does wonders for yourself.

It will help you sleep better.

It will help you find it easier to relax.

You may even have those moments where you get excited about the future. Acceptance does wonders for you. But it also does wonders for the people you love.

Seriously.

When you live a life of acceptance, you can love the people around you the way they need to be loved. When you are so busy thinking about your past mistakes or how much you dislike where you are right now, you become kind of self-involved.

And by kind of, I mean A LOT.

If your mind can't stop thinking about all the things you wish were different, or how that person hurt you once, or why you didn't get that promotion, you really have no room in your mind for anyone else.

If you're married, it's particularly important, because your spouse didn't choose to spend their life with a mopey, sad, and frequently irritated person. I know this because when I act mopey, sad, and irritated, my wife reminds me that *that* person was not present on our wedding day.

This isn't to say she doesn't support and love me through the tough times. She's awesome at that. But she's also awesome at saying what a lot of spouses don't say.

She is fine with pointing out errant nose hair.

She keeps me from looking disheveled when I walk out the door by pointing out the stain on my vest that I clearly missed.

I was about to head out to a big meeting with potential clients yesterday when she stopped me. I honestly loved what I had on and was feeling confident and ready. But she said, "You're changing that shirt, right?" I had missed the giant sweat stains in the armpits. I went upstairs and changed. (Nothing tells a client you're confident more than armpit stains.)

I didn't like it, but she was right.

When I was in my "bad" place, having a hard time letting go of the past and moving on, she called me on it with conviction and love.

She made clear on a few occasions that the mopeyness was fine for awhile, but she couldn't keep living with that. She even said, "I'm okay with it 50% of the time—but it can't be this *all the time*."

This was her way of saying I needed to get my crap together.

She broke down in tears one night because my lack of accepting who I was and where I was had her living in fear for the future. She was filled—overwhelmed by, even—with feelings she didn't deserve to have because I could not let go of the past. Her husband was not doing his job in the marriage because he was so busy thinking about himself and wishing things were different.

God makes pretty clear that when we love someone, we have to give up a lot of our rights to selfishness. "Love is not selfish" is actually right there in the list of verses of what love is. I know because I performed about twenty weddings this year, and this verse is always a popular one at weddings.

If you love someone, you don't have the right to live in a way that is focused on you. Whether you are married or single, God has strong feelings on how we get to treat someone if we say we love them. He made the list of all the things that love is.

"Love is mopey."

"Love is sad."

And "love is irritable" are not on the list.

The people you love (your spouse, family, friends) deserve the best you. The "best you" is not the one who gets angry and frumps around the house and reads through old emails to relive the glory days (yes, I have done just that, to my regret).

The "best you" is the one who figures out how to move beyond the past, doesn't jump down people's throats, and can walk around with confidence and assurance that everything is going to be okay.

*A word of advice: this may take some *professional help*. I can give you some pointers, having been there myself, but I can't help you work through the big stuff. If you can't seem to let go of anger or selfishness and are hurting the ones you love because of it, I want to say it's ok.

Go see a therapist.

Talk it out, get it out, and let them guide you into your best you.

After twenty years of marriage, my wife knows when I'm being my best me. So, I'm slowly learning that Paul's words to the Romans are exactly what God wants from me. And it's what He wants from you, too. Paul says that love must be sincere.

Sincere is defined as "free from pretense or deceit; proceeding from genuine feelings."

So be real.

Be genuine. And give the people who love you the love they deserve, and that God wants you to give.

After reminding the Romans to be sincere in their love, Paul later wrote to the Corinthians. The list of what love is, which is what God wants from you and me, and how He wants us to love others.

Love is patient and kind.

Love is not jealous or boastful or proud or rude. It does not demand its own way. It is not irritable, and it keeps no record of being wronged. It does not rejoice about injustice but rejoices whenever the truth wins out.

Love never gives up, never loses faith, is always hopeful, and endures through every circumstance.

Love endures through *every* circumstance.

Your best and worst. Especially your worst.

Stop thinking that you're okay and get help if you need it.

You'll be amazed at how your relationships will change and get better. You may even think, "Wow! Everyone is so much nicer!"

Surprise! They really aren't any nicer—but changing your perception of yourself helps you see them as they deserve to be seen and loved the way that God wants you to love them.

Which means *you* are nicer. And that's good.

Love must be sincere.
Romans 12:9a

I Can See Clearly Now
(But the Rain Isn't Gone)

If you live in a place where there are lots of clouds, you come to appreciate the sudden, glorious moment when blue sky appears, and you can actually feel the warmth of the sun on your face.

If you live in a place where it's always sunny (like Philadelphia, ha ha), you may not understand. Sure, you get your moments of clouds and rain, but when you live in perpetual grey for nine months out of the year, when the sun shines, everything changes.

It's like an old friend you totally forgot about suddenly shows up and takes you on vacation.

(By the way, if any old friends are reading this and would like to do that, I'm totally ready to go. It's been raining off and on all week, and I'm really getting tired of it. Who has two thumbs up and is ready for some sunshine? *This guy!*)

When we are in the middle of a time of struggle or facing tough times, we live in the days of rain and grey. Caught up in the middle of the storms of life, it's hard to remember that there are days of sun and warmth.

Who wants to accept the constant cloud cover?

Even people who choose to live in Seattle get tired of it. There's a reason as soon as the sun shines, everyone puts on shorts.

I have a small window above my desk.

I can't see much out of it beyond a few branches from a maple by the side of the house. On a cloudy day, there's nothing but a solid hue of grey with a bit of even greyer shadowing.

In the time I've been working on this book, I've seen day after day of grey sky. It's literally the opposite of that song "I Can See Clearly Now:" "Look all around, there's nothing but grey sky!"

As another day of the grey threatened to engulf the view, something happened the other day. The clouds began to part, and I got a hint of blue sky and warm yellow-orange light.

The sun was basically shouting, "I'm still here!"

Your life of storms and clouds and rain is not going to be here forever. Beyond the clouds the sun is shining, and sometimes we just need to accept that what we are going through is just a storm to be weathered.

The sun doesn't cease to shine because the clouds are out. And God doesn't cease to shine His light into our lives just because we are facing a storm.

In the book of Samuel, which is actually mostly about the life of King David, we see the only person God ever named as someone "after His own heart" nearing the end of his days.

David wrote the Psalms of praise, the Psalms of anger, the Psalms of travel, the Psalms of confession. He's been writing about God and the way He works nearly all His life.

And at the end of his life, David sang these words about God. They are beautiful and should be included in the Psalms so more people memorize them. But since they aren't, here you go.

The Psalmist's last song:

"He is like the light of morning at sunrise
on a cloudless morning,
like the brightness after rain
that brings grass from the earth." (2 Samuel 23:4, NIV)

This is what God is doing.

He is light that shines on both bright and dark days, and He is always working. Like the sun that never stop shining, God never stops working. He is shining His light into your life even now, whether your day is bright or dark.

And like the "brightness after rain," He will bring the good thing into your life. Your life, which has seemed dark and cloudy and barren, will brim and overflow with life again.

Remember, we may not see Him doing His work, but you know that He is.

You know He is because everything hasn't completely gone wrong, in spite of the grey.

If the sun stopped shining behind those clouds, life as we know it would cease to exist. But it doesn't—it never stops working, even though we can't see it.

God's love and grace and mercy continue to shine the light above the grey of our current circumstance. He will give you the strength you need for this day and He will ensure you have what you need for this day, too.

As the prophet Jeremiah once wrote about God's compassion—His grace and mercy—it's *new every morning.*

Every day the light returns, every day His mercy and grace and joy come back. You can't exhaust it, you can't wear it out. Even if you go to bed feeling sad and defeated and merciless and graceless and it seems like your world has no joy, when you wake up the next day, God surprises you and says, "You can have it all again today. Look! I'm giving it to you—will you take it?"

That's kind of the key here. Unlike the sun, which shines whether you like it or not, God will not force Himself on you. He *wants* to give you these things. He wants to give you a new day, a new chance, a new opportunity for joy and peace. But ultimately, whether or not you get those things is up to you.

Will you take it from Him?

Will you accept what He offers?

New every morning.

Brightness after rain.

Light of morning.

Let these words encourage you today.

Take what He is offering you and let each day be new and fresh and filled with light, even if you're struggling with a lack of sunshine and light. If your day is grey and you're feeling down and a little gray, take heart and be encouraged. God is still doing something new. He is still faithful to complete that good work He started in you.

The clouds will *not* last forever.

The sunshine does come back.

So, take heart.

And a final word of caution: if you don't like rain or grey skies, don't live in Seattle. If you've only visited in the summer, I want you to know: the weather is lying to you.

Now we see but a poor reflection as in a mirror; then we shall see face to face.

1 Corinthians 13:12a

You Have What You Need

The other day, I sat down in a state of depressed overthinking. Have you ever done that? You spent too much time thinking about things—your situation, your emotions, your family—and suddenly you realize you thought *way too much.*

You overthought everything from breakfast that morning to the decision you made to talk back to your 6th grade teacher. (If you're reading this, Mrs. Okamoto, I apologize. You deserved far better than my sarcastic response.)

I was in a bad state.

In spite of trying to get past the hurt of a recent wound, I was instead nursing it and allowing it to become a hot bitter mess. When confronted with that realization by Robyn, I was stunned.

She was right.

Here I was, a former pastor, fully engaged in being filled with something I know to be unhealthy and hurtful.

After a little confession and introspection, I was forced to realize I'd spent a year of my life being angry at people who moved on the day after I left.

Because I'm a moody artistic type, this only caused me to think even more deeply.

This is never good.

My head can be a very dark and scary place.

(Don't judge me, because I know yours is just as bad.)

And then I just grew sad and down and worried that I'd wasted all that time and was I doing what I was supposed to be doing? Was I just wasting more time pursuing—whatever it is that I was doing?

By the end of the day I was sitting with my wife and brother and sister-in-law. I was being very woe is me, and they were speaking good things in to me. You've probably had a moment like that, where you say a lot of things about how awful you are and people say, "No, you're great!" or "Yes, you are, and here's how you fix it."

It's a good and bad moment at the same time, and if you do it in person (and not on social media) it can actually be quite healthy to hear what people who actually care about you think about the current state of your affairs.

I asked a question about what I was doing and who I am, and where am I going, anyway? There's a song from the musical *Sweet Charity* that I'm sure I started singing. It's called "Where Am I Going?" and I've often sung this song at these moments in my life. If you decide to go listen to it, look for the Original Broadway Cast version sung by Gwen Verdon.

So here I was on that night, looking back at my life, at every career I've had, the things I've done and created, I wondered how it all fit together. That's when my family looked at me as if I was crazy. "It all fits together! You've been telling stories *this whole time.* You are a *storyteller!*" they said.

This is a key part of acceptance.

You can let go of your past and jump into your future when someone helps you realize that you already have everything you need to be happy or successful or content or joyful. The skills and things you learned years ago are part of the very things that make you *you.*

What are those things? Figure them out.

Because all of them contributed to your story and to who you are *right now.* You can probably pick up a few skills if you need to, but you already have what you need. (If you need some additional reassurance, read *Oh, the Places You'll Go* by Dr. Seuss.)

I didn't realize it until that moment, though.

God had already prepped me for this. The thing I was having such a hard time accepting was the very thing that God had spent the last 20 years of my life getting me ready to do.

There are no accidents when you realize that God's providence is working out every small detail for the betterment of *you.* He promises this throughout the Bible.

"And we know that God causes everything to work together for the good of those who love God and are called according to his purpose for them." (Romans 8:28, NLT)

This means all the stuff you've gone through and experienced, the good and bad, the wonderful and heartbreaking will be used by God for your *good*. (Remember that word from earlier? It's the same here. Good that is wonderful and awesome and fantastic, even if you may not realize it at the time.)

Having a hard time believing that? I understand it. I still struggle with wondering how God can use everything in my current life and situation to work together for my good. I know I've been called according to His purpose—but what does that call say, exactly?

I know how it feels, and so does God. Which is why another verse reminds us that we need to *"Trust in the Lord with all your heart and lean not on your own understanding."* Which is actually incredibly good advice. My own understanding creates hot messes for me and everyone in my life. God's understanding? Well, He's made clear His thoughts are beyond anything I can even begin to comprehend.

The verse ends with *"In all your ways submit to Him, and He will make your paths straight." (Proverbs 3:5-6, NIV)*. Which is a not so subtle reminder to not try and control what is happening. Let go and let Him do what He wants to do.

He gave you everything you needed to get started on the day you were born. He has spent the last several years of your life getting you ready for the next thing!

So get ready to embrace it.

Stop stewing in pity.

Stop embracing anger and bitterness.

God created you for something so much bigger and better, and He has been working on you to get you ready for a very long time.

It's time to accept it.

You have what you need.

You don't need to be like anyone else or have what they have. You have *exactly* what you need, because that's the way God works.

It took me nearly a year to the day for me to understand and realize it, so I hope you catch on sooner. If you think you don't have what it takes to achieve the dreams and goals He's placed in your heart, you are in for a very big surprise.

For we are God's workmanship, created in Christ Jesus to do good works,
which God prepared in advance for us to do.
Ephesians 2:10

Going-to-the-Sun Road

I wish I could say that life would get easier after you let go and begin to live with acceptance. "Thanks for reading. This book has a pain free guarantee!"

But as Westley says in *The Princess Bride*, "Life is pain, Highness! Anyone who says otherwise is selling something."

It's not going to get easier, because that's not the way things work.

The minute you begin to accept one thing, you'll see the deficiency in another area that you need to work on. Once you've accepted something else, you discover that the trouble with that one went super deep. Life will not simplify or get jollier just because your outlook has changed.

If anything, it will take more work on your part to move past new hurts more quickly, embrace change more frequently, and—here's the kicker—be a light for those who are now going through the very things you were facing last month. (Or an hour ago.)

It reminds me a bit of traveling one of the most beautiful stretches of road in the United States. It's at Glacier National Park, and it's called "Going-to-the-Sun Road."

It's a marvel of engineering, a beautiful example of using a highway to compliment the land as opposed to running roughshod over it.

The road is built right into the cliff.

It's a pretty incredible thing.

If you go slow enough, you can literally touch the side of the mountain as you drive. (In fact, so many people do it I'm surprised there aren't more traffic accidents around there.) The reason it reminds me of acceptance—at this stage in the game—is because being able to reach out and touch the wall is pretty cool, but it's absolutely game-changing to anyone who hates mountain highways.

My wife hates mountain highways.

One summer we were on a long road trip with my parents and grandmother. My mom and I had mapped everything out and planned the roads between different sights and national parks. So we chose a scenic byway in Utah for one leg of the trip.

Turns out it was was just a road carved across the top of a mountain—with nothing but sheer drops on either side. I was driving so it didn't bother me, but holy cow. I didn't realize until then how much the combination of cliffs and heights and minivans mess my wife up.

(You should check it out if you're ever in Utah driving between Bryce Canyon National Park and Capitol Reef National Park.)

Which explains why, when she saw the beginning of Going-to-the-Sun Road, Robyn was not exactly thrilled. And by not exactly thrilled, I mean she was freaking out. She was doing breathing exercises we'd learned during birthing class and she was clutching the door handle so tightly I was afraid she was going to snap it right off.

But as we started up the road, two things happened. I didn't go very fast, and she realized she could do something she'd never been able to do on mountain cliff roads.

She could reach out and touch the side of the cliff, warm from the summer sun. This began to change everything. The road didn't get exactly easier, but it sure was much more comfortable for her to navigate. I could tell by her face the road went from being "We-Are-Going-To-Die Road" to the more idyllic actual name.

Every time she got nervous, we slowed down, and she put her hand on the cliff wall.

Your life isn't going to get easier.

You're going to have similar roads on your journey.

There are going to be moments along the road.

Moments where you may want to panic.

Times when you feel stress.

Days when you can't seem to get out of your head.

Acceptance allows you to reach out and touch the wall and be reminded that you've survived, and you'll be okay. Even as the climb gets harder and higher, you can still take comfort and a little bit of calm by leaning into something that is steady and constant and never out of reach.

Even better than the cliff wall is the love of a God who is just as steady, just as constant, and even closer. He is always near, always ready to remind you that you will be okay. He will keep you from heading off the cliff of worry or fear. When the next tough time comes, accept that it's happening and lean into the steady, unfailing arms of God.

Remember the words of David from Psalm 121?

The Lord himself watches over you!

The Lord stands beside you as your protective shade.

The sun will not harm you by day,

nor the moon at night.

The Lord keeps you from all harm

and watches over your life.

The Lord keeps watch over you as you come and go,

both now and forever.

God stands beside you, my friend.

He walks with you and journeys with you! He's not going to let you fall off the cliff. Heck, he's not even going to let you get too hot! Whatever sort of harm you may be fearing right now, remember that He will keep you from it.

He will not let it take you down into destruction and ruin.

He will watch over you no matter where you may go.

If you're a bit scared of heights or travelling fast or being in a place where if a wandering cow gets in the way you can plummet to your doom, don't drive Utah State Highway 12.

If you really want to test the metaphor above, go visit Glacier National Park and get ready for a beautiful and amazing journey. Hug the wall of Going-to-the-Sun Road.

Drive slow enough to touch it as you drive by, and marvel at the way the road moves and twists and turns with the cliff wall. (If you're already planning your trip, just a word of advice: you'll have to go in the summer, since it's snowed over most of the year.)

And if you just want to stay closer to home, remember: the road is not over, the journey is still going. Hard times will still come, and God will still be there for you to lean on.

Yet this I call to mind and therefore I have hope:
Because of the Lord's great love we are not consumed,
for his compassions never fail.
They are new every morning; great is your faithfulness.
Jeremiah 3:21-23a

It's Better than the Box. Trust Me.

A life of acceptance is not a life of resignation.

I want to make that clear.

Letting go is *not* giving up.

Accepting who you are today doesn't mean you are fated to be this way forever. Are you unhappy with your current job? Do you know you need to lose weight? Do you wish you spent less time at work? Acceptance doesn't mean, "Oh well, I give up."

If you need to get a different job, start working on it. If you need to lose weight, make the healthy choices to ensure it happens. If you need to work less, *stop working so much.*

Acceptance is being okay with things as they are right now, in this particular moment.

Letting go of the hurts and wounds of the past, letting go of the bitterness, letting go of the always wishing for things to be different will give you great freedom.

You'll discover things about yourself and your situation that you couldn't see before. You may realize you have skills and talents you have left unused. You may discover you are more deeply loved than you remember.

Even better, you may wake up one morning and feel the peace and hope that God promised because you are finally resting in His promises.

Remember, the whole purpose of accepting who you are today is so you'll be ready for who you will be tomorrow. None of us are created to stay where we are today. But if we believe the only way to be happy or content is to wish for something we don't have, we are missing out on the blessings that God promises each day.

Remember that verse from Jeremiah? The one that reminds us, "They are *new* every morning."

Each new day brings *new* mercies, *new* blessings, *new* opportunities to see what He is doing in our lives. If we don't let go of what we had before, we can't open our hands and hearts to what He is offering us today.

When we live this way, we're like the kid who unwraps a big box on Christmas Day. As a parent, you know what's inside the box. You put the latest, coolest, and greatest toy inside.

But instead of seeing it, the child can't stop talking about how awesome the box is and how he can't wait to play with the box.

He's busy rhapsodizing about this incredible box, left over from a previous Amazon delivery, and all you can think about is the fact that he's missing the real gift. And if you try to point it out, the child gets mad and angry, "But I *love* this box!"

God is as frustrated with us as the parent is with the box-obsessed kid. He's trying to hand us a beautiful thing for this day, and all we can think about is the beat-up old box from a previous delivery. He's giving you so many things you need *right now*, and all you can see is what you had yesterday, or the day before. You can only see what you *don't have.*

You can't see the gift of today because you're too busy thinking about all the stuff that happened in your life previously. Or all the worries you have because of something that hasn't even happened tomorrow.

"I'm giving you a brand-new Xbox!" God says.

And our response isn't, "Holy cow! That's awesome! Thank you, God!" No, our answer is, "No thank you, I can't stop thinking about the Atari I had when I was seven. It had this super sweet game of Pong on it."

(You can use a metaphor that works better for you, if you're not into videogames. I write what I know.)

Sadly, there's another variation that's just as bad when you're not living a life of acceptance. Let's say you're not the kid who can only see the box. You open the gift, pull out the really cool new present (interesting that the word means the same as *right now*, right?), hold it for a second or two, then set it down and look around and say, "Okay, but what I really can't wait to get is _____."

If you're a parent, you understand.

You found a great gift that your child has been talking about for months. She hasn't stopped talking about how cool it would be to own this particular thing.

"If I only get this one thing, it will be all I need in life!" she cries. (My kids talk in dramatic extremes. They get that from their mother, I'm sure.) So we scour the internet, pay the extra shipping when it's not available on Amazon Prime, and have it ready for Christmas Day.

She opens it up and talks about how she loves it, how we are the best parents ever. We feel like we won the holiday! And then she says, "But I found this really cool thing yesterday—can I buy it with the money I get from Grandpa?" Parental eye roll and frustration commences and then we deliver a lecture on being content to a kid who literally just got the "one thing" she wanted most in life.

We do this all the time with God.

We pray and ask for "just this one thing" to make us happy.

We ask for God to give us better health or deeper friendships.

We ask for a good day at work or a better night's sleep.

And when we start the next day and God gives us *just that*, we say, "Thanks, but what I *really* need is [insert cool new thing here]." Don't you think that makes Him a little bit crazy?

Acceptance is being happy with the gifts we are given today.

Life is going to be filled with good and bad and wonderful and awful. You're going to struggle at times, while other times you will be on top.

There will be moments of bright sunshine and many others of grey clouds. Unwrap today's gift, whatever it is, and be thankful. Accept that it was given to you for a reason by a God who knows you better than anyone, and who loves to give you the desires of your heart.

Let go of the box from the past.

Let go of the wishing for something better tomorrow.

Open your hands to today. Open your heart to this moment. Open your life to what is happening right now and embrace who you are, where you are, and what you are doing today.

God promises to give you exactly what you need today.

Maybe a new and better career is ahead of you.

Perhaps you'll find a way to mend a broken relationship from the past. Maybe you'll lose the weight or discover your talent was there, ready to be used all along. Perhaps you'll help someone else and renew your faith in God's promises and gifts.

I hope that your future is truly incredible. I truly do.

But what matters most is right now, for this is all we truly have promised to us: *today*. Accept today for what it is. Accept yourself for who you are—*right now*.

Because one day you're going to wake up and God is going to say, "Okay, you're ready for this new thing. Let's go!"

When this happens, my prayer is that will find yourself in the same place as Bilbo Baggins the morning he wakes up and realizes he needs to join the dwarves on their journey. With great excitement and joy, he races through Hobbiton and someone yells, "Mr. Bilbo! Where are you going?"

Bilbo shouts back with glee, "I'm going on an adventure!"

That morning will come for you.

And a whole new journey, a whole new experience—a whole new life to accept—will have arrived.

Let go of all the things of yesterday. Put the luggage down, no matter what it holds.

It may be great memories or big-time hurts. It may be things you love or things that cause you to wince when you think about them. Whatever they are, you won't be able to finish the journey if you keep holding them.

So put them down.

Accept who you are today. Because when you do that, you will be ready for all the things He has in store for you tomorrow. All you have to do is let go.

Happy journey, my friend. I'll meet you there.

If they obey and serve him, they will spend the rest of their days
in prosperity and their years in contentment.
Job 36:1

Afterword

There you have it.

Thirty chapters about what it means to let go and begin living a life of acceptance. It's been a year since I started this process, and I'm not done. Honestly, I'm not. I still struggle with accepting myself and where I am and what God has in store for me. Writing these words have helped me—and I hope they help you, too. Because I get it.

I still have a lot to accept about myself.

I still miss some of the things I used to do and be.

And that's okay.

You still do, too.

I know you will struggle with letting go.

You'll have days where you feel like you've nailed it and days when you feel like you've fallen right back into the worst of yourself.

You are going to have grey days and long nights and sometimes you'll forget to choose your response and need someone who loves you to talk you from the edge. I know because it happens to me, too.

When that happens, remember.

Remember your focus matters.

Remember that "If only…" won't get you anywhere.

Don't forget to take a break now and then, and make sure you find any bitterness and dig it out. Acceptance is something we need to do daily, because we are always growing, always changing, and we always have something new to accept about our lives and ourselves.

So let me offer you one last encouragement and reminder: it's okay. Nothing that happened today surprises God.

Nothing.

He knows the contents of your bank account, the status of the job application, the results of the doctor's tests. He knows you will struggle in your response to it.

But that's okay.

He doesn't look at you and say, "Jeez! Can't you see what I'm trying to do? Come on! I *knew* this was gonna happen. You have got to start *trusting* me!"

No, He does the exact opposite.

He sees where you falter and fail and loves you anyway. He knows your doubts and sends encouragement. He hears your worries and offers you hope. His mercies that are new every day are for everyone, even the broken and wounded and struggling.

Rest in that realization and know that *He will not let you go.*

Knowing that He has hold of you and will never let you falter or fall should give you the courage to do what you need to do. He will not let go, but you can!

Remember the words of David, from Psalm 121:

I look up to the mountains—
    does my help come from there?
My help comes from the Lord,
    who made heaven and earth!
He will not let you stumble;
    the one who watches over you will not slumber.
Indeed, he who watches over Israel
    never slumbers or sleeps.
The Lord himself watches over you!
    The Lord stands beside you as your protective shade.
The sun will not harm you by day,
    nor the moon at night.
The Lord keeps you from all harm
    and watches over your life.
The Lord keeps watch over you as you come and go,
    both now and forever.

Stop clinging, stop grasping, and stop holding on. Your journey will be great. Your road is watched over constantly by the One who set you on your path.

You can do it.

Start accepting where you are today so you can be ready for who you will be tomorrow. It may not be easy, but it will be worth it. Let's discover what comes next together.

Let's go for it, okay?

Open your hands. Relax your muscles. Trust God.

Just let go.

ABOUT THE AUTHOR

DUANE S. MONTAGUE
has been writing for a long time,
publishing his first magazine article at age 12.
He has worked for the Walt Disney Company, Microsoft,
and two of the largest churches in the Pacific Northwest.
He is a writer for David C. Cook's *Action Bible Curriculum*.
He is currently the Chief Storyteller at Thinks, LLC,
a company that helps people and
businesses across the United States tell their stories.

He has been married to Robyn for 20 years.
They have four awesome kids and travel to
Disneyland and America's National Parks as often as possible.

He is also the author of
Resting Merry: Discovering Joy & Peace at Christmas
What About Baptism? A Guide for Kids & Their Parents
The Bear Necessities Series

You can find more of his writings and works online at
duanesm.com & thinksinc.org

On social media, find him on
Twitter @dsmontague
Instagram @dsmontague
Facebook: dsmontague